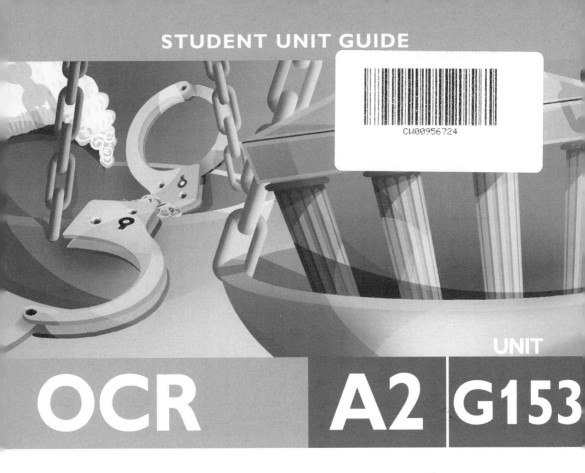

STUDENT UNIT GUIDE

UNIT

OCR   A2 G153

Law

Criminal Law

Chris Turner and Leon Riley

Philip Allan Updates, an imprint of Hodder Education, an Hachette UK company, Market Place, Deddington, Oxfordshire, OX15 0SE

Orders

Bookpoint Ltd, 130 Milton Park, Abingdon, Oxfordshire, OX14 4SB
tel: 01235 827720
fax: 01235 400454
e-mail: uk.orders@bookpoint.co.uk
Lines are open 9.00 a.m.–5.00 p.m., Monday to Saturday, with a 24-hour message answering service. You can also order through the Philip Allan Updates website: www.philipallan.co.uk

ISBN 978-0-340-97619-7

First printed 2009
Impression number 5 4 3 2 1
Year 2013 2012 2011 2010 2009

This guide has been written specifically to support students preparing for the OCR A2 Law Unit G153 examination. The content has been neither approved nor endorsed by OCR and remains the sole responsibility of the authors.

Typeset by Phoenix Photosetting, Chatham, Kent
Printed by MPG Books, Bodmin

Hachette UK's policy is to use papers that are natural, renewable and recyclable products and made from wood grown in sustainable forests. The logging and manufacturing processes are expected to conform to the environmental regulations of the country of origin.

Contents

Introduction

■ ■ ■

Content Guidance

■ ■ ■

Questions and Answers

Introduction

About this guide

This study guide is written for students following the OCR A2 Law course and covers the specification content of **Unit G153: Criminal Law**. The selection of the topics in this module is designed to give students a sound introduction to the essential elements for proving criminal liability, both for crimes requiring proof of criminal intent and for crimes of strict liability, where criminal intent is not necessary. The unit also examines attempted crimes. It covers the main substantive homicide offences, including murder, the special and partial defences to murder often referred to as voluntary manslaughter, and the different types of involuntary manslaughter where the specific intent required for murder cannot be proved despite the unlawful killing. The main defences for avoiding criminal liability are covered, including insanity, duress, non-insane automatism and intoxication. The unit also examines the non-fatal offences against the person, including common assault and battery, actual bodily harm, wounding and grievous bodily harm, as well as the defences of self-defence and consent. Finally, the unit covers the substantive property offences of theft, robbery and burglary.

There are three sections to this guide:
- **Introduction** — this section gives advice on how to use the guide, some learning strategies, some hints on planning revision, a reminder of the assessment criteria and how to achieve them, and also an explanation of what the exam paper is about and the skills needed to complete it successfully.
- **Content Guidance** — this section sets out the specification content for Unit G153, and the key knowledge for successful completion of the exam. It is broken down into subsections in the same way as the specification and provides a structure for your learning. Where cases or statutes are referred to, you will need to study these in more detail for a fuller understanding.
- **Questions and Answers** — this section provides sample answers to typical examination questions on each topic area. Each question is followed by an A- and usually a C-grade answer. Examiner comments show how marks are awarded or why they are withheld.

How to use this guide

The Content Guidance section covers all the elements of the Criminal Law specification, breaking down each topic into manageable sections for initial study and later revision. It is not intended to be a comprehensive and detailed set of notes for the unit — the material needs to be supplemented by further reading from textbooks and by your own class notes.

At the end of each topic section, you may find it useful to compile a summary of the factual material under appropriate headings. Ideally, you should incorporate additional material drawn from a number of sources: classroom teaching, textbooks, quality newspapers, law journals and legal websites. When you have finished compiling your notes, you can tackle the questions in the third section of the guide. Read the questions carefully and answer them fully. You should then read the sample A-grade answers and compare these with your own answers to identify where you could have gained more marks in order to achieve a higher grade. Compare your answers with the C-grade answers too, in order to get an indication of how well you are performing. The examiner comments will help you to understand what factors can limit your marks and how you can attain the higher grades.

Learning strategies

A2 is very different from AS and more is required of you in the examinations. While the good knowledge and understanding you may have of the various topics studied during your course is still important at A2, you will need a greater depth of under-standing and will need to learn many more cases. For this reason, you must keep a clear and accurate set of notes. Another significant difference at A2 is that you are expected to have better-developed critical ability, meaning that you will need to show that you can discuss the law at length in the essay questions for Section A and apply the law effectively to factual situations in the problem questions for Section B.

You should employ an effective learning strategy as follows:
- Try to take notes in class in a logical and methodical way — don't just write down everything that the teacher says.
- Make sure that you read your notes again after each class — don't leave it too long or the information will not be fresh in your mind.
- If you don't understand something in your notes, read about it in your textbook or ask your teacher. Make sure you correct your notes so that you can understand them.
- Do all the reading that your teacher suggests and also try to read around the subject to build up greater knowledge and understanding. If you have spaces in your class notes, you can add additional information from your reading. If not, you should rewrite your notes to incorporate it.
- Build up a good understanding of the principles of law that come from the individual cases and try to remember the case names by testing yourself frequently.
- Use a legal dictionary so that you become familiar with all the appropriate legal terminology.

Revision planning

Revision is not the same as learning. All of the learning strategies mentioned above should have been covered during the course and you should have a complete and accurate set of notes when you begin your revision. If you have to learn the material from scratch before the exam, then you are putting extra pressure on yourself.

There are various rules for good revision practice that you should follow:

- Organise your material before you begin. You will be revising more than one subject, which will have many topics. It will help your revision process if you have separate folders for each subject. Use folder dividers for individual topics, so that you can turn straight to the topic you wish to revise.
- Organise your time effectively. Thirty minutes preparing a revision timetable will save you a lot of time later on. Divide the time you have available by the topic areas. Identify how many times you can revise them and create a chart.
- Use effective revision aids to help compress the subject matter or put it into visual form to make the process simpler and less time consuming. Examples are key facts charts, mind maps, flowcharts and diagrams.
- Make revision cards on all the leading cases.
- Ask your friends and family to test you on important knowledge.
- Practise past papers. The more familiar you are with the style of questions that you can expect, the more confident you will become in answering them in the exam. Tackling problem questions in particular will help to build your understanding, since the law makes more sense when it is applied to factual situations.
- Do your revision in short bursts. The longer you sit looking at your notes in one session, the more likely you are to get bored and not take anything in. Take plenty of breaks between sessions.

Assessment objectives

Assessment objectives (AOs) are the measures against which examiners test your knowledge, understanding and legal skills. They are common to AS and A2 units and are used by all boards offering AS/A2 Law. They are intended to assess a candidate's ability to:

- AO1 — recall, select and develop knowledge and understanding of legal principles accurately by means of example and citation, i.e. your ability to remember the appropriate law, including cases or statute where appropriate.
- AO2 — analyse legal material, issues and situations, and evaluate and apply the appropriate legal rules and principles, i.e. your ability to engage in a balanced discussion, offering points of criticism in essays, and to apply legal rules to factual situations in problem-style questions.
- AO3 — present a logical and coherent argument, communicating relevant material in a clear and effective manner, using appropriate legal terminology, i.e. your ability to give legal information and to discuss or apply it clearly, as well as to spell, punctuate and use grammar accurately.

Remember that in OCR A2 exams there are five levels of assessment, while in AS exams there are only four. This means that you have to show more knowledge and better analysis or application skills in order to reach the highest mark level.

For AO1, this means that as well as demonstrating that you have well-developed knowledge, as you did for AS, it must be wide ranging.

For AO2 you must show a high level of analysis or application, and not just analyse the more obvious points or apply the obvious law, as would have been expected of you at AS.

When you sit AS examinations, you have only completed 1 year of the A-level course. After 2 years, you are expected to have gained more knowledge and to have developed better skills. Don't think that, just because you got a good grade at AS, you will automatically do so at A2.

There is also an extra level for AO3, so your communication skills should have improved, and for the highest level you will be expected to write with few, if any, errors of spelling, punctuation or grammar.

The examination

Unit G153 is made up of three sections and in 2 hours you have to answer one question from a choice of two in each section. Questions in Sections A and B are worth 50 marks, made up of 25 marks for AO1, 20 marks for AO2 and 5 marks for AO3. Section C questions are worth 20 AO2 marks. It is suggested that candidates spend 50 minutes on each of the Section A and B questions, and 20 minutes on Section C.

Section A contains essay-style questions, where you are expected to show your knowledge of the topic areas and also to analyse and/or evaluate. You must be able to identify the critical purpose of the question asked, to engage in a balanced discussion looking at both sides of an argument, and finally to reach conclusions resulting from that discussion.

Section B questions involve legal problem solving. You will be provided with a factual scenario and you will then have to identify the areas of law that could be used to resolve the issues that arise from the scenario. In criminal law, this means that you will need to identify offences that may arise from the facts, as well as possible defences. With fatal offences, problems are less likely to involve multiple issues because there are only a few substantive offences in the specification content. You are likely to see problems on murder, with causation as a major issue. Issues concerning attempt could also be included. Questions on diminished responsibility and provocation are common too, and do not forget that there are often different possibilities arising from the same set of facts. Involuntary manslaughter is often examined as a problem-solving question.

Section C questions are objective questions, where you are called on to use your understanding of core legal principles and pure legal reasoning to validate or invalidate four definitive statements about a small scenario.

Planning is an important part of achieving high marks in any examination. In the case of essays for Section A, remember the importance of structuring your answer. Your answer should include:
- an introduction identifying what the question is asking
- a balanced discussion using cases, sections of Acts and legal principles in support of your answer
- a reasoned conclusion deriving from your discussion

Structure is also important in the problem-solving questions for Section B. You must:
- identify, for each individual aspect of the problem, the key facts on which resolution of the problem is based
- define the appropriate law
- apply the law to the facts
- reach sound conclusions based on your application of the law

For the objective questions in Section C, remember that both your reasoning and your conclusion are vital for high marks. Remember also that for this section only you do not have to cite cases or statutes in your answers.

Remember also to:
- read the question thoroughly, so that you are certain what it is asking for
- plan your answer briefly at the start of the exam to ensure you only use relevant information and do not miss anything out
- always use law (cases or statutes) in support of your arguments for essays or in your application for problem questions
- avoid excessive use of the facts of cases — it is the principle that is important
- make sure that you answer the question set

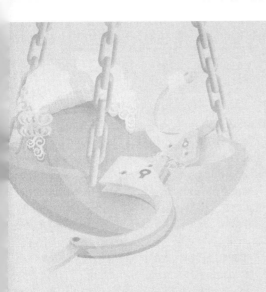

Content
Guidance

The material covered in G153 of the Criminal Law option is divided into six sections. The first is concerned with the essential elements of crimes and is vital to the understanding of all substantive offences. In this section of the Criminal Law specification content, it is absolutely vital for you to gain a good understanding of some fairly difficult concepts. The second covers attempted crimes. The third covers the major crimes of homicide, including murder, partial defences to murder contained in the Homicide Act 1957 (an area often referred to as voluntary manslaughter) and involuntary manslaughter (killing that lacks the necessary criminal intent for murder). This section reinforces the first, as it includes many of the cases that you will have learned when covering the essential elements of crimes. The fourth section is concerned with the main defences to crimes. Some are incapacitating defences, including insanity, non-insane automatism and intoxication. Others are based on excuse, such as duress and mistake. The fifth section covers the non-fatal offences against the person, including the main defences to these. The offences range in seriousness from assault and battery to wounding or grievous bodily harm, requiring ulterior intent. The final section covers offences against property. This includes the basic theft offence and its key elements and the more specific property offences of robbery and burglary. The areas covered in Unit G153 are:

Principles of criminal liability
Actus reus
- Voluntary conduct
- Omissions
- Causation

Mens rea
- Direct intent, oblique intent and foresight of consequences
- Recklessness
- Gross negligence
- Specific intent and basic intent
- Transferred malice

Strict liability

Attempted crimes
Fatal offences against the person
Murder
- Actus reus and mens rea

Voluntary manslaughter
- Special and partial defences: diminished responsibility, provocation

Involuntary manslaughter
- Constructive (unlawful act) manslaughter
- Gross negligence manslaughter
- Reckless manslaughter

General defences
- Insanity
- Non-insane automatism
- Duress of threats, duress of circumstances
- Necessity
- Intoxication

Non-fatal offences against the person
Assaults
- Assault and battery
- Assault occasioning actual bodily harm

Wounding and grievous bodily harm
- Wounding
- Grievous bodily harm

Defences
- Self-defence and prevention of crime
- Consent

Offences against property
- Theft
- Robbery
- Burglary

Principles of criminal liability

Actus reus

All crimes, with the exception of those identified as 'strict liability', require proof of both a criminal act and a criminal intention. This requirement comes from the maxim *'actus non facit reum, nisi mens sit rea'*, meaning that an act by itself will not make a person guilty unless the mind is guilty.

The *actus reus* is the factual part of the crime and is often referred to by criminal lawyers as the 'external element' of the crime. The criminal act can involve different categories of fact (some crimes involve all of these but sometimes one alone is enough):

- **Conduct.** This refers to the active part of the *actus reus*, i.e. what the defendant does. Sometimes the *actus reus* can *only* be based on conduct, e.g. perjury. There does not always have to be a positive act, and in some circumstances, a failure to act or an omission can lead to criminal liability. In rarer circumstances, a mere 'state of affairs' can be sufficient.
- **Circumstances.** This refers to the context in which the act becomes a crime. Sometimes an act may be legitimate and not criminal at all if the circumstances are different, e.g. consent to an assault that occurs in a sporting context, where the laws of the game have been followed.
- **Consequences.** Some crimes are called 'result' crimes because whatever the act, the crime is incomplete until a specific result occurs, e.g. homicide offences such as murder and manslaughter require a death.

Voluntary and involuntary conduct

The *actus reus* of a crime only exists where the defendant's conduct is voluntary. As a result, if the defendant's act or omission is beyond his or her control, then there is no criminal liability (*Kay* v *Butterworth*, 1945). Since voluntary conduct must also be conscious conduct, if the defendant is unconscious or unaware, then *actus reus* is missing. In this case the defence of non-insane automatism may apply. However, this automatism is difficult to demonstrate satisfactorily, as illustrated by *Broome* v *Perkins* (1987).

The Law Commission in the Draft Criminal Code suggested an alternative definition whereby a person is not guilty of an offence if:

- he or she acts in a state of automatism, i.e. the act is a reflex, spasm or convulsion, or it occurs while the person is in a condition of sleep, unconsciousness, impaired consciousness or otherwise, depriving him/her of effective control of the act
- the act or condition is the result neither of anything done or omitted with the fault required for the offence, nor of voluntary intoxication

Sometimes, however, a defendant can be convicted even in the absence of voluntary conduct because he or she falls within a 'state of affairs' that is prohibited by the criminal law *(R v Larsonneur*, 1933). This seems unfair because the defendant has no control over the state of affairs and there appears to be an absence of *actus reus*. However, the principle has been approved more than once *(Winzar v Chief Constable of Kent*, 1983).

Omissions as *actus reus*

On the whole, English law requires a positive act. There is no provision for a 'Good Samaritan' law, so it is generally not possible to impose liability for a failure to act. However, because of the presence of duty situations in English law, it is possible to be criminally liable for a failure to act in certain defined circumstances, where this failure amounts to a breach of a specific duty to act.

The situations are limited but the *actus reus* can include an omission where a duty to act arises:
- under a contract, e.g. *R v Pittwood* (1902)
- from specific relationships such as parent and child, e.g. *R v Gibbons and Proctor* (1918), or doctor and patient, e.g. *Airedale NHS Trust v Bland* (1993)
- from a voluntary assumption of care for another, e.g. *R v Stone and Dobinson* (1977)
- from a statutory duty to act, e.g. *R v Dytham* (1979)
- as a result of the defendant's prior dangerous conduct, e.g. *R v Miller* (1983)

Actus reus and causation

Since the *actus reus* is based on the defendant's voluntary conduct, causation can be an issue in determining criminal liability in 'result' crimes such as murder or manslaughter, when the identity of the party responsible for the actual outcome is called into question.

Causation is measured in two ways:
- **Factual causation.** The question of the defendant's criminal liability is determined on the basis of the 'but for' test, i.e. but for the defendant's criminal act or omission would the victim have suffered the damage? If the answer is no, then the defendant is criminally liable. If something else is the cause of the damage, then the defendant is not liable *(R v White*, 1910).
- **Legal causation.** This is a more complex issue and concerns whether or not the defendant can be said to be legally responsible for the result. For instance, in *R v Pagett* (1983), the victim was killed by police gunshots during a siege. However, the defendant had used the victim as a human shield during a gunfire exchange with police officers in a dark alleyway and so was legally the cause of the victim's death.

A number of factors need to be considered in determining causation:
- whether the defendant's act is a sufficiently substantial cause *(R v Adams*, 1957)
- the effect of cumulative causes — compare *R v Benge* (1865) with *R v Armstrong* (1989)
- the effect of intervening events — generally, if a *novus actus interveniens* (a new intervening act) breaks the chain of causation, it relieves the defendant of liability

because the intervening act is then the real cause; however, merely switching off the life-support machine of a victim declared brainstem dead does not break the chain of causation (*R* v *Malcharek*, 1981)
- the defendant must 'take his victim how he finds him', so that the defendant is not excused where, for example, a Jehovah's Witness has refused a subsequent blood transfusion (*R* v *Blaue*, 1975)
- the fact that subsequent negligent medical treatment only breaks the chain of causation if it is the actual operative cause of death, and the defendant's act or omission can no longer be seen to be connected to the result (*R* v *Jordan*, 1956); the preferred position is that which occurred in *R* v *Smith* (1959) and *R* v *Cheshire* (1991)

Mens rea

In criminal law (with the exception of strict liability offences), a defendant can be guilty of an offence only if he or she can be shown to have acted with criminal intent. This criminal intent is referred to as *mens rea*.

Mens rea is potentially complex as there are different levels and the required *mens rea* varies from crime to crime.

Sometimes certain aspects of the *mens rea* are not only a state of mind but also descriptive of other aspects of the *mens rea*, e.g. a deception by deliberate or reckless intent, or there may be an ulterior intent, e.g. a reckless wounding with the intent of committing grievous bodily harm.

The external elements of the crime (the *actus reus*, or the conduct of the accused) and the *mens rea* constitute the separate ingredients of a crime. In each criminal case, the prosecution is obliged to prove at least the minimum level of criminal intent appropriate to the individual crime.

There are three types of criminal intent (depending on the individual crime):
- intention
- recklessness
- gross negligence

Intention

Intention, sometimes referred to as 'full-blown intention', is the highest level of *mens rea*. In *R* v *Mohan* (1976), the court suggested that this form of intention occurs when the defendant decides to bring about a prohibited consequence, irrespective of whether he or she also *desires* to bring about that consequence. The Law Commission in the Draft Criminal Code has suggested that the definition should be: 'a person acts intentionally with respect to a result when he or she acts either in order to bring it about or being aware that it will occur in the ordinary course of events.'

There are two types of intention:
- direct intent
- oblique intent

Direct intent

Direct intent is straightforward. It occurs when the result is actually desired by the defendant. In this sense, it is immaterial that the desired result is achieved, since an inchoate offence is still possible, e.g. attempted murder. Motive is also irrelevant, since this is not the same as intent (*Yip Chiu-cheung* v *R*, 1994).

Oblique intent

Oblique intent (also known as 'foresight intent') is where intent has to be inferred from the evidence. This covers the situation where the consequence is foreseen by the defendant as virtually certain, although it is not desired for its own sake, and the defendant goes ahead with his/her actions anyway. Inevitably, this type of intent is measured against foresight of those consequences, i.e. how likely the result was to occur. For this reason, it has caused many problems. Many of the cases that deal with how oblique intent can be measured are murder cases, and the House of Lords has reached many confusing and often conflicting interpretations.

At one time, foresight was measured objectively according to the standards of the reasonable person and classed as equivalent to intent (*DPP* v *Smith*, 1961). However, this was unsatisfactory because it negated any need to show the defendant's mental state and so it was remedied by s.8 of the **Criminal Law Act 1967**. This states that a jury, in determining whether a person has committed an offence:
- *shall not* be bound in law to infer that he intended or foresaw a result of his actions by reason only of its being a natural and probable consequence of those actions but
- *shall* decide whether he did intend or foresee that result by reference to all the evidence, drawing such inferences from the evidence as appear proper in the circumstances

Foresight was then linked to probability in *Hyam* v *DPP* (1975), but on a split decision 3:2 with each judge giving different reasons for the result, thus confusing the issue still further. This approach was rejected as being too broad and ambiguous in *R* v *Moloney* (1985). Lord Bridge's direction was that intent could only be inferred where death or serious injury was a 'natural consequence' of the defendant's act and the defendant foresaw that this was the case.

However, this narrowed the test too far and was still ambiguous, so Lord Scarman developed guidelines for judges and juries in *R* v *Hancock and Shankland* (1986), suggesting that foresight was not a legal test but only factual evidence from which to infer intent. He stated that the greater the probability of a consequence, the greater the likelihood that it was foreseen, and that the more likely it was foreseen the more likely it was intended. This test was redefined into a model direction by Lord Lane in *R* v *Nedrick* (1986). The court made the following points:
- If a consequence is desired, then as a matter of law it is intended.
- Where foresight of consequences is absent, then as a matter of law there is no intent.

- The degree of foresight in between these points is a question of fact for the jury to decide, with guidance from the judge, in order to determine existence or otherwise of intention. (Foresight is not the same as intention but only evidence from which intent can be inferred.)
- In those cases where intent needs to be inferred, the jury should ask two questions:
  — How probable was the consequence which resulted from the defendant's act?
  — Did the defendant foresee those consequences?
  The jury should only then infer intention if death or serious injury was a virtual certainty and the defendant appreciated that this was the case.

This 'model direction' was initially rejected by the Court of Appeal in *R v Woollin* (1997), but the Court was overruled by the House of Lords. While the Court of Appeal disapproved of the use of the two questions from *Nedrick*, the model direction was approved with the word 'find' being used in place of the word 'infer'. Subsequently, the Court of Appeal in *R v Matthews and Alleyne* (2003) has confirmed that foresight of consequences is only evidence of intention, and it is not automatically intention.

Recklessness

Recklessness is a lesser mental state than actual intention, so it is not the same as desiring the consequences, as would be the case with direct intent. It is arguable, however, whether recklessness is merely a step away from oblique intent, and the distinction may not be so easy to define.

The defining feature of recklessness is the taking of an unjustified risk, i.e. the defendant appreciated the existence of the risk but nevertheless carried on and took it. In determining whether the defendant was reckless, the jury would need to decide:
- how likely the risked consequence was
- the social utility of the acts which created the risk
- the practicability of any possible precautions that could have been taken to avoid the risk

Recklessness has traditionally been measured in two different ways:
- objective recklessness
- subjective recklessness

Objective recklessness

Objective recklessness stems from the case of *R v Caldwell* (1981). It works on the basis of asking whether a reasonable person in the defendant's circumstances would have appreciated that the risk existed. If so, the defendant could be guilty on the basis of recklessness, regardless of whether he or she actually did recognise the risk.

This objective standard of recklessness, however, had the obvious potential to cause injustice, such as in the classic example of *Elliott v C* (1983). *Caldwell* concerned criminal damage, but objective recklessness caused even greater controversy when applied in other areas, e.g. causing death by reckless driving (*R v Lawrence*, 1982). Therefore, it was later held that it could only be applied in cases of criminal damage.

Now, following *R v G and another* (2003), the House of Lords has overruled *Caldwell* and only subjective recklessness can be used.

Subjective recklessness

Subjective recklessness derives from *R v Cunningham* (1957) and is based on asking whether or not the defendant realised the existence of a risk but nevertheless went on to take it. If so, then the defendant is guilty.

Subjective recklessness is now the only type of recklessness accepted by the courts. It had, in any case, already been accepted in all offences where the definition of the offence included the word 'maliciously' (*R v Savage*, 1992).

One problem has been identified in relation to subjective recklessness: the so-called lacuna, or loophole. Here, the defendant might claim that he or she honestly did not believe that there was a risk, or that he or she had eliminated the risk, in which case, if this is accepted, there can be no conviction. However, successful cases demonstrating a lacuna are rare (*R v Merrick*, 1996), as the point on which the defendant is mistaken must exclude any possibility of risk (*R v Reid*, 1992).

The Draft Criminal Code favours use of subjective recklessness only.

Gross negligence

Gross negligence applies only in the context of manslaughter. Negligence is a civil concept, where objective standards are common and are measured against the reasonable person, and where the standard of proof is lower than for criminal law. Consequently, there is some conceptual overlap with *Caldwell* recklessness and some of the same difficulties arise.

Gross negligence can include:
- contemplating a risk and wrongly concluding that it does not exist
- recognising a risk and taking inadequate steps to avoid it

Gross negligence is now the proper test in manslaughter (*R v Adomako*, 1995):
- Liability first depends on the existence of a duty owed by the defendant to the victim.
- The test is whether the defendant's behaviour is so negligent in all the circumstances as to justify a conviction for manslaughter.
- This test is one purely for the jury to decide.

One potential benefit of gross negligence is that it may make it easier to bring a charge of corporate manslaughter.

Specific intent and basic intent

It is also possible to classify intent in criminal offences as either:
- basic intent, where the *mens rea* does not extend past the *actus reus*, e.g. rape
- specific intent, where the *mens rea* does extend past the *actus reus*, e.g. murder (where the unlawful killing must be carried out with malice aforethought), or theft

(where the appropriation of the property belonging to another person must be done dishonestly and with the intention permanently to deprive another of that property)

In the case of crimes of basic intent, the necessary *mens rea* can be either intention or recklessness. However, with crimes of specific intent, the *mens rea* requires either direct intent or oblique intent, or that one element of the *mens rea* goes beyond the *actus reus* (e.g. the intention permanently to deprive in theft).

Another possible distinction between basic intent and specific intent is that intoxication may provide a defence for crimes of specific intent, but it can never provide a defence for crimes of basic intent, because there is recklessness in becoming intoxicated.

Transferred malice

A defendant may be liable for a criminal offence, even though the victim is different to the one intended, or the consequence occurs in a different way (*R* v *Latimer*, 1886), in which case the *mens rea* transfers to the other victim.

However, the *mens rea* cannot be transferred to a substantially different offence (*R* v *Pembliton*, 1874).

The coincidence of the *actus reus* and the *mens rea*

Generally, both the act and the mental state must be contemporaneous for an offence to be committed. However, the courts have been quite liberal in their interpretation of the coincidence of the two, obviously for pragmatic reasons and also to ensure that justice prevails over technicality.

In this way, the courts have accepted that there is still coincidence of the *actus reus* and the *mens rea* in the case of:
- continuing acts (*Fagan* v *Metropolitan Police Commissioner*, 1969). These are generally those cases where the *mens rea* is not formed until after the conduct of the *actus reus* has begun and the link is that it continues (*R* v *Kaitamaki*, 1984).
- cases amounting to single transactions (*R* v *Thabo Meli*, 1954). These are generally where the *actus reus* is not complete at the time there is *mens rea* (*R* v *Church*, 1966 and *R* v *Le Brun*, 1991).

Strict liability

Strict liability simply means that there is no requirement to prove a mental element in respect of one or more areas of the *actus reus*. However, the concept is not that straightforward and it is often easier to show *how* the principle of strict liability operates than *when* it operates. It is generally an unclear and imprecise area.

Strict liability can be complicated because one or more of the general defences may be available. Certainly in the case of strict liability offences deriving from statute, the statute itself may indicate available defences. An obvious example is the due diligence defence that is common in offences involving consumer protection.

On this basis, strict liability should not be confused with absolute liability, where even a lack of voluntary conduct would not prevent liability (*R* v *Larsonneur*, 1933). It is possible, however, that the defendant could be liable merely for his or her blameless inadvertence (e.g. s.4 of the **Road Traffic Act 1988**, driving with excess alcohol in the blood), which applies regardless of the reason for it.

The majority of strict liability crimes are statutory, so the offences are mostly regulatory. However, some strict liability offences can involve imprisonment (*Gammon (Hong Kong) Ltd* v *AG of Hong Kong*, 1984).

There are a few common-law strict liability offences. The three main ones are public nuisance, criminal libel and blasphemous libel (*R* v *Lemon and Gay News*, 1979).

Strict liability becomes a problem when a statute is silent on the issue of *mens rea*. The general presumption is that a crime always requires *mens rea*, unless the contrary is expressly stated by Parliament (*Sweet* v *Parsley*, 1970). However, this is a refutable presumption (*Pharmaceutical Society of Great Britain* v *Storkwain*, 1986) and it is possible to be convicted of a strict liability offence even though the defendant is unaware of the fact of committing the wrong (*Cundy* v *Le Cocq*, 1884). To complicate the area still further, strict liability offences have been identified in the past with an element of *mens rea* (*R* v *Prince*, 1895, although this case was not followed in *B* v *DPP*, 2000).

Factors significant in establishing strict liability

The modern approach of the courts to strict liability was put clearly by Lord Scarman in *Gammon (Hong Kong) Ltd* v *AG of Hong Kong* (1984):

(1) There is a presumption of law that *mens rea* is required before a person can be guilty of a criminal offence.
(2) The presumption is particularly strong where the offence is 'truly criminal' in character.
(3) The presumption applies to statutory offences, and can be displaced only if this is clearly, or by necessary implication, the effect of the statute.
(4) The only situation in which the presumption can be displaced is where the statute is concerned with an issue of social concern.
(5) Public safety is such an issue.
(6) Even where the statute is concerned with such an issue, the presumption of *mens rea* stands, unless it can be shown that the creation of strict liability will be effective to promote the objects of the statute by encouraging greater vigilance to prevent the commission of the prohibited act.

It is difficult to say when the courts will identify that an offence is strict liability. However, the following guidelines be used:

The statutory context — the wording of the Act
There is no guarantee as to which words will lead to strict liability, but there are some patterns:

- The words 'permitting', 'allowing', 'knowingly' or 'intentionally' usually imply that there is a requirement of *mens rea* because they clearly indicate an awareness (compare *James and Sons* v *Smee*, 1955 with *Green* v *Burnett*, 1955).
- Where the word 'cause' is used, common sense often dictates that there is no requirement for *mens rea* (*Wrothwell* v *Yorkshire Water Authority*, 1984).
- The word 'possession' usually requires some form of knowledge (*Warner* v *Metropolitan Police Commissioner*, 1969).
- It may be that the absence of a particular word means that strict liability will be accepted (*Kirkland* v *Robinson*, 1987).

The social context — crimes and quasi-crimes

The House of Lords in *Sweet* v *Parsley* (1970) identified that crimes should be distinguished from regulatory offences that are for the convenience of the public. Crimes always need *mens rea*, whereas regulatory offences rarely do. Clearly, the more dangerous the activity involved, then the more likely it is that the courts will apply the presumption of *mens rea* (*R* v *Howells*, 1977). Further, offences may be accepted by the courts as strict liability for pure reasons of public policy (*R* v *Blake*, 1997).

Strict liability offences can often apply to regulate:
- sale of food and drink
- licensing of activities
- protection of the environment
- supply of drugs and pharmaceuticals
- road traffic activities

The severity of the punishment

Usually, the greater the available punishment the more likely it is that *mens rea* is required, but this is not an absolute test (*Gammon (Hong Kong) Ltd* v *AG of Hong Kong*, 1984). Even crimes attaching quite severe punishment have been accepted as strict liability (*R* v *Champ*, 1981).

It may be that a court needs to look at all possible pointers, a fact that reinforces the view of the Law Commission that, when enacting new offences, Parliament should be clear in the Act whether or not the offence is strict liability (*B (a minor)* v *DPP*, 2000).

It is common in modern statutes to include certain defences to strict liability offences. An example of these is the due diligence or third party defence that appears in consumer protection statutes such as the **Trade Descriptions Act 1968** and the **Misuse of Drugs Act 1971**.

Arguments in favour of strict liability

- helps to protect the public
- is easier for the police and for bodies such as Trading Standards to enforce
- can act as a deterrent to bad business practice
- creates recognisable standards
- reduces time and cost of court appearances
- follows the fault principle in tort

- reduces the evidential burden
- is always possible for Parliament to provide a defence where appropriate
- levels of blame can be accounted for by sentencing

Arguments against strict liability

- denies people the chance to state a case
- does not necessarily raise standards
- may punish people who have, in fact, taken proper care
- people may take the blame for another individual's wrongdoing
- can offend human rights principles

Suggested reform

The Law Commission has suggested reforms that are contained in the Draft Criminal Code. It says that 'every offence requires a fault element of recklessness with respect to each of its elements other than fault elements, unless otherwise provided'. The main effect of such a reform would be that no offence would be taken as being strict liability unless Parliament had expressly stated it as being so in the Act.

Attempted crimes

An attempt is where the defendant has the necessary criminal intent and sets out to commit the crime but fails to actually complete it. The definition in s.1(1) of the **Criminal Attempts Act 1981** states:

> ...if with an intent to commit an offence to which this section applies, the person does an act which is more than merely preparatory to the commission of the offence, he is guilty of attempting to commit the offence...

A charge of attempt is not possible in the case of summary offences, nor can there be an attempt to conspire, aid, abet, counsel or procure.

One area that proved controversial for a while was the area of 'attempting the impossible'. Under s.1(2) of the Act: 'A person may be guilty of attempting to commit an offence...even though the facts are such that the commission of the offence is impossible.' This overruled a previous unsatisfactory common-law rule that made an attempt that was a legal or factual impossibility beyond prosecution (*Haughton* v *Smith*, 1973).

The section originally caused some difficulty of interpretation for the courts but was eventually resolved correctly by the House of Lords in *R* v *Shivpuri* (1987), which overruled its incorrect interpretation of the previous year in *Anderton* v *Ryan* (1986).

Section 1(3) also clarifies the issue:

> In cases where, apart from this subsection, a person's intention would not be recognised as having amounted to an intent to commit an offence, but if the facts of the case were as he believed them to be, his intention would have been so regarded, then...he shall be regarded as having an intent to commit that offence.

Attempts and the *actus reus*

Under the **Criminal Attempts Act 1981**, the key element of the *actus reus* is that the act is 'more than merely preparatory to the commission of the offence'.

This obviously requires interpretation. Originally there were a number of ways of establishing this under the common law. At one time, the test was merely one of proximity (*Comer* v *Bloomfield*, 1970). It was also often measured by the 'last act test' (*R* v *Eagleton*, 1855). A simple test was whether the defendant had reached 'a point from which it is impossible to return' (*DPP* v *Stonehouse*, 1978). However, under the current law, the defendant need not have committed the last act or reached a point of no return (*A-G's Reference (No. 3 of 1992)*, 1994). Probably the most satisfactory question to ask is whether the defendant has carried out an act that shows that he or she actually tried to commit the offence, or whether he or she has merely put himself or herself in a position where he or she is ready or equipped to commit the offence (*R* v *Geddes*, 1996).

Nevertheless, the words 'more than merely preparatory' have created many grey areas, as can be seen by comparing the results in *R* v *Gullefer* (1987) and *R* v *Campbell* (1991) with those in *R* v *Boyle and Boyle* (1987) and *R* v *Kenneth Jones* (1990).

Attempts and the *mens rea*

The *mens rea* is normally the same as for the main offence. However, it may require a greater degree of intent (*R* v *Walker and Hayles*, 1990). In attempted murder, for instance, it is necessary to show a higher degree of *mens rea* than in the offence itself. Intention to kill is required for attempted murder — intention to cause grievous bodily harm is not sufficient. A defendant must intend a strict liability offence, even though that in itself would have no *mens rea* (*Alphacell Ltd* v *Woodward*, 1972).

Intention may be inferred from foresight of consequences, where the result in question is virtually certain to occur and the defendant knows this (*R* v *Walker and Hayles*, 1990).

In some instances, recklessness has been accepted as appropriate *mens rea*, despite older authorities maintaining the contrary (*R* v *Khan*, 1990). Certain developments have shown a trend towards a general rule of reckless attempts, although that was never intended (*A-G's Reference (No. 3 of 1992)*, 1994).

Fatal offences against the person

Murder

Murder is a homicide offence and is obviously a result crime (however badly the accused has harmed the victim, if the victim does not die, homicide has not occurred).

Unlike most crimes, murder is still a common-law offence. This is technically important only as an issue in drafting indictments. However, the definition of murder is the one set out by Sir Edward Coke in the seventeenth century and it is arguable whether this is satisfactory today. The elements of the offence from the definition are that a person of sound mind over the age of 10 unlawfully kills a reasonable person actually in being and 'residing under the King's/Queen's peace' with malice aforethought, either expressed by the defendant or implied by law. Formerly the definition also required that the victim should die within a year and a day. This has now been removed as the result of the **Law Reform (Year and a Day Rule) Act 1996**. However, reference must be made to the Attorney General in the case of deaths occurring 3 years or more after the attack, and where the defendant has already been convicted of a lesser offence.

As with all crimes, each separate ingredient of the offence must be proved. All ingredients of the offence except malice aforethought are *actus reus* and apply to all homicides.

Malice aforethought alone is the *mens rea* of murder. If malice aforethought cannot be proved, the offence cannot be murder, even though it involves an unlawful killing.

It is, of course, possible for an accused to avoid conviction because he or she can claim a complete defence that negates either the *mens rea* or the *actus reus*. On certain other occasions, both the *actus reus* and the *mens rea* of murder can be proved, but the accused is able to claim one of the special and partial defences identified in the **Homicide Act 1957** and referred to as 'voluntary manslaughter'. In these instances, even though murder can be proved, if the plea is accepted, the charge is reduced to manslaughter.

Murder is classed at the highest level of wickedness. As a result, on conviction it receives a mandatory life sentence. In contrast, in the case of other homicides there may be discretionary sentencing available to the judge. In recent times, several leading judges, as well as law reformers, have called for the mandatory sentence for murder to be removed and for discretion to be used in imposing a sentence that reflects the crime.

The *actus reus* of murder

The *actus reus* of murder is appropriate for homicides generally. There are four aspects:
- a description of the perpetrator
- the unlawful killing

- a description of the victim
- the jurisdiction of the court

Coke's definition referred to 'a man of sound memory and the age of discretion'. This merely means that the accused is not mentally incapacitated, and is therefore legally sane, or is too young, i.e. under the age of 10, when criminal intent cannot be formed. This definition refers to women too, as well as to children over the age of 10.

A killing must be unlawful for a homicide to occur. By definition, this means that some killings are lawful, and if a killing has a lawful justification it will not be a criminal offence. Lawful killings include:
- a killing carried out in self defence
- (formerly) where the killing was a lawful capital punishment
- where an enemy alien is killed in time of war (although this does not include a prisoner of war)

The victim of a homicide is described as 'a reasonable person actually in being'. This sounds complex and is due to the archaic language used in the original definition. In simple terms, the issue is whether the victim is a living human being at the time of the alleged killing, i.e. a human being who is recognised in law as being alive. Problem areas can concern when life begins, such as in the cases of *R* v *Brain* (1834), *R* v *Senior* (1899) and *A-G's Reference (No. 3 of 1994)* (1997). Similar problems arise over the issue of when life ends (although, at this point, the major issue is really causation), e.g. *R* v *Malcharek* (1981), *R* v *Steel* (1981), *R* v *Blaue* (1975), *R* v *Adams* (1957), *R* v *Cox* (1992), *Airedale NHS Trust* v *Bland* (1993) and *Re A (Conjoined Twins)* (2001).

The requirement that the accused should be 'residing under the King's/Queen's peace' merely refers to the jurisdiction of the court to try the offence. Jurisdiction is very wide, since an English court may try any UK citizen for a murder that he or she has committed anywhere in the world.

The *mens rea* of murder

The *mens rea* of murder is defined as 'with malice aforethought express or implied'. Again, this definition appears to be complex and confusing, because of the archaic language used in Coke's definition.
- 'Malice' in this context does not refer to the usual dictionary definition of 'spite', and could include even mercy killing (*R* v *Adams*, 1957).
- 'Aforethought' in this context is not necessarily the same as premeditation, so it can include spur of the moment killings (*R* v *Church*, 1966).
- Express malice simply means the intention to kill.
- Implied malice is the intention to cause grievous bodily harm (this is defined as meaning really serious harm).

Murder is a crime of specific intent, so recklessness can never be sufficient *mens rea* for it. As we have already seen, the necessary intent can be shown either where there is direct intent or where there is oblique intent.

Direct intent is relatively straightforward, and what must be shown is that the defendant desired the actual consequences. Here, foresight is not really an issue (*R* v *Michael*, 1840). However, as we have already seen, murder can still occur where there is oblique intent, of which foresight of consequences is the traditional measure. It does not matter what consequence the defendant actually desired, as long as it can be shown that the actual consequence was foreseeable. Problems have then occurred in determining the part to be played by foresight. At one time, it was measured objectively (*DPP* v *Smith*, 1961) but this was unsatisfactory, since it seemed to negate the need for *mens rea*, and as a result this was amended in s.8 of the **Criminal Law Act 1967**.

Subsequently, foresight of probable consequences and intent were held to be interchangeable (*R* v *Hyam*, 1974), but again this was clearly unsatisfactory, as well as confusing.

After this, only clear intent was held to be sufficient, and foresight of consequences was identified as being the only evidence from which intention could be inferred (*R* v *Moloney*, 1985).

Now, the House of Lords has accepted a workable definition that intention should not be inferred from foresight unless 'death or serious bodily harm was a virtual certainty' (*R* v *Nedrick*, 1986, approved in *R* v *Woollin*, 1998 HL).

Voluntary manslaughter

Voluntary manslaughter is a general term used to refer to the special and partial defences provided by the **Homicide Act 1957**. The key feature is that murder is being charged and both the *actus reus* and *mens rea* of murder can be proved. The defendant generally has no complete defence available and so a conviction is possible.

However, the defendant is able to claim one of the special and partial defences made available by the **Homicide Act 1957**. If any of these is successfully claimed, this has the effect of reducing the charge from murder to manslaughter and removing the mandatory life sentence.

The defences include diminished responsibility (s.2) and provocation (s.3).

Diminished responsibility

The defence of diminished responsibility came about because of the inadequacies of the M'Naghten rules on insanity. The defence has no basis in common law (as provocation does) but is entirely the creation of statute in s.2 **Homicide Act 1957**. It applies only as a partial defence to murder (unlike insanity, which applies generally to all crimes), and is designed to replace insanity, which was seen as sometimes unjust or unsatisfactory.

Diminished responsibility can be claimed where the defendant is 'suffering from such abnormality of mind (whether arising from a condition of arrested or retarded development of mind or any inherent causes or induced by disease or injury) as substantially impaired his mental responsibility'. The defence is much wider than insanity and is in many ways much more realistic.

There are three specific elements that must be shown for a successful plea:
- **The abnormality of the mind.** This is determined by the jury, although medical evidence is taken into account. There is no particular definition, although Lord Parker in *R v Byrne* (1960) suggested that it was 'a state of mind so different from that of ordinary human beings that a reasonable man would term it abnormal'.
- **The cause of the abnormality.** This must be one of those identified in s.2, which is in fact very wide and covers both internal and external factors. For instance, while ordinary rage would not be sufficient, uncontrollable impulses could be (*R v Byrne*, 1960). It could also include abnormality caused by such factors as battered wife syndrome (*R v Hobson*, 1997) and severe reactive depression (*R v Seers*, 1984), so the list of causes is confusing to psychiatrists as well as to laymen. Drunkenness cannot be a cause, though alcoholism might be (*R v Tandy*, 1988). In *R v Dietschmann* (2003), the House of Lords identified that drink and the abnormality of mind might both play a part in impairing the defendant's mental responsibility, in which case the jury should determine whether, despite the effect of the alcohol on the defendant's mind, the abnormality still substantially impaired his or her mental responsibility.
- **Substantial impaired mental responsibility.** Again, this is a question of fact for the jury to decide, which can be achieved with very little evidence, or fail where there is a wealth of evidence.

Two significant reforms are suggested in the Draft Criminal Code:
- Intoxication should be kept entirely separate from diminished responsibility.
- The defendant should only have to raise evidence of diminished responsibility and it should then be for the prosecution to disprove it.

Provocation

Provocation was originally a common-law defence and a successful plea depended on actions. Words alone were insufficient to succeed in the defence (*Holmes v DPP*, 1946). The common-law definition was 'some act done by the dead man to the accused which would cause a reasonable person and actually does cause the defendant a sudden and temporary loss of control' (Devlin J in *R v Duffy*, 1949).

The defence is now found in s.3 **Homicide Act 1957**:

> Where, on a charge of murder, there is evidence on which the jury can find that the person charged was provoked (whether by things done or by things said or by both together) to lose his self-control, the question whether the provocation was enough to make a reasonable man do as he did shall be left to be determined by the jury...and the jury shall take into account everything according to the effect...it would have on a reasonable man.

The trial judge decides if there is any evidence indicating provocation (*R* v *Acott*, 1997). The judge then leaves the question of whether the defendant was actually provoked to the jury and it is for the prosecution to disprove (*R* v *Cascoe*, 1970).

Members of the jury must ask themselves two questions:

- Was the defendant provoked so that he or she actually lost self-control? (This is the subjective test as in the prior common law, *R* v *Duffy*, 1949.) This should be a sudden and temporary loss of control, so that a cooling off period between the provocation and the loss of control means that the defence is likely to fail (*R* v *Thornton*, 1992 and *R* v *Ahluwalia*, 1992).
- Would a reasonable person have reacted in the same way? (This is the objective question that has proved to be problematic.) This originally caused problems where the defendant had characteristics that the reasonable person would not have (e.g. impotence (*R* v *Bedder*, 1954)). Following *R* v *Camplin* (1978), the age, sex and other relevant characteristics of the accused can be taken into account in determining how the reasonable person would have reacted. Relevant characteristics have been extended to include battered women's syndrome (*R* v *Hobson*, 1997), addiction (*R* v *Morhall*, 1995) and immaturity and attention seeking (*R* v *Humphries*, 1995). However, mental conditions such as brain disorders and depression should not be taken into account, as they are more appropriately dealt with under diminished responsibility (*R* v *Luc Thiet Thuan*, 1997). *R* v *Smith (Morgan James)* (1998) held that abnormal characteristics of the accused may be relevant not only to the gravity of the provocation, but also to the ability of the reasonable person to deal with the provocation. In *R* v *Holley* (2005) the Privy Council rejected this approach, and in *R* v *James*, *R* v *Karimi* (2006) the Court of Appeal identified that *Holley* and not *Smith* was the appropriate test.

Provocation has become an extremely wide defence and almost any characteristic can now be taken into account. It has been argued that *Smith* (1998) reduces the self-control that is to be expected of the defendant to an unacceptably low level. The Law Commission has suggested that either the defence should be abolished or the wording of the section should be changed to:

> A person who, but for this section, would be guilty of murder is not guilty of murder if (a) he acts when provoked (whether by things done or said or both and whether by the deceased person or by another) to lose his self-control and (b) the provocation is, in all the circumstances (including any of his personal characteristics that affect its gravity), sufficient ground for the loss of self-control.

Involuntary manslaughter

Involuntary manslaughter is unlawful killing with insufficient *mens rea* for murder, so it covers those areas where the prosecution is unable to show malice aforethought. In voluntary manslaughter, the defendant did intend to kill or to cause serious harm to the victim, but can claim a special and partial defence provided by statute. In involuntary manslaughter, on the other hand, the defendant is arguing that he or she did not intend to kill, and this is the 'involuntariness' referred to.

However, there is still some measure of culpability, otherwise it would not be an unlawful killing. As a result, involuntary manslaughter is, in some ways, an imprecise area. It can be both complex and diverse as it covers all of those killings which fall between murder and accidental or justified killing. It can also be committed in a number of ways.

Constructive manslaughter (unlawful act manslaughter)

This type of manslaughter is based on the notion of 'constructive malice': if the death occurred during the commission of an unlawful act, the prosecution need only prove *mens rea* of that unlawful act in order to convict for manslaughter. This is why it is also called 'unlawful act' manslaughter.

The major definition was given by Lord Salmon in *DPP* v *Newbury and Jones* (1977), stating that the accused would be guilty of manslaughter if it could be proved that he or she 'intentionally did an act which was unlawful and dangerous and that the act inadvertently caused death'. This approved the judgement of Edmund Davies J in *R* v *Church* (1966): 'the unlawful act must be such as all sober and reasonable people would inevitably recognise must subject the other person to at least the risk of some harm resulting therefrom.'

The prosecution needs to prove two things, i.e:
* the existence of an unlawful act committed by the defendant
* the unlawful act must be dangerous

The existence of an unlawful act committed by the defendant

An omission would not be sufficient for constructive manslaughter (*R* v *Lowe*, 1973). The act itself must be unlawful rather than a lawful act that has been carried out unlawfully (*Andrews* v *DPP*, 1937), so a death caused by a civil wrong would be insufficient (*R* v *Franklin*, 1883). The unlawful act must be carried out with the appropriate *mens rea* (*R* v *Lamb*, 1967) and there can be no conviction if the act leading to the death was done with lawful justification (*R* v *Scarlett*, 1993). However, intoxication is not an excuse for carrying out an unlawful act that leads to an inadvertent death (*R* v *Lipman*, 1970).

One line of cases that creates apparent difficulties concerns defendants who supply victims with drugs, who subsequently die from taking the drug. The unlawful act identified is usually maliciously administering a noxious substance contrary to s.23 of the **Offences Against the Person Act 1861**. A problem here is proving causation. If the defendant only supplies the drug and does nothing more, there can be no conviction for constructive manslaughter (*R* v *Dalby*, 1982). If the defendant injects the victim, there can be a conviction (*R* v *Cato*, 1976). In *R* v *Kennedy* (1998), it was held that the defendant could be convicted for filling the syringe with which the victim then injected himself, resulting in death, the unlawful act being assisting the victim in his unlawful act. This view, however, was held to be wrong in *R* v *Dias* (2001). The House of Lords in *R* v *Kennedy* (2007) held that the victim's voluntary act of injecting himself broke the chain of causation between the defendant's supply of the drug and the victim's death. In *R* v *Rogers* (2003), an actual act of assisting in the injection, for instance by applying a tourniquet, was found to be an unlawful act that led to a conviction.

The unlawful act must be dangerous

This means that there must be a risk of harm, which reasonable and sober people would recognise as a risk (*R* v *Church*, 1966). There must be a risk of physical harm rather than mere emotional disturbance (*R* v *Dawson*, 1985). However, where a reasonable person would realise that, in the circumstances, the victim's general frailty would lead to a risk of physical harm, there can be a conviction for a resulting death (*R* v *Watson*, 1989). It does not matter that the defendant did not recognise the risk: the test is not 'did the accused recognise that it was dangerous?' but 'would all sober and reasonable people recognise its danger?' (Lord Salmon in *DPP* v *Newbury and Jones*, 1977).

Originally, it was also considered that the unlawful act should be directed at the victim. The original test was that if the unlawful act were only an indirect cause of death, there was no manslaughter (*R* v *Dalby*, 1982). However, this test is outdated and a better test is whether the harm is directly linked to the unlawful act so that it could be aimed at properly (*R* v *Goodfellow*, 1986). It is also possible that manslaughter can result from an intentional, unlawful and dangerous act done to another (*A-G's Reference (No. 3 of 1994)*, 1997).

Gross negligence manslaughter

Traditionally, the courts accepted manslaughter caused by gross negligence. This depended first on the defendant owing the victim a duty of care. The original definition was contained in *R* v *Bateman* (1925):

> ...the facts must be such that...the negligence of the accused went beyond a mere matter of compensation...and showed such disregard for life and safety as to amount to a crime against the state and conduct deserving of punishment...

Gross negligence was distinguished from recklessness in *Andrews* v *DPP* (1937):

> ...simple lack of care as will constitute civil liability is insufficient...reckless suggests indifference to risk, whereas the accused may have appreciated the risk and intended to avoid it and yet shown such a high degree of negligence in the means adopted to avoid as would justify a conviction...

There was, at one time, a dispute about whether recklessness or gross negligence should be applied and whether the appropriate test ought to be objective or subjective. If the correct test were subjective, then foresight of injury would also be important (*R* v *Pike*, 1961). However, if the test were objective, then it would be the standards of the jury that should apply (*R* v *Seymour*, 1983). The House of Lords then accepted the test of objective recklessness from *R* v *Caldwell* (1982) and *R* v *Lawrence* (1982) as the appropriate test. This appeared to be the end of gross negligence manslaughter, since Lord Roskill argued that Caldwell recklessness should be applied throughout the criminal law, confirmed again by Lord Roskill in *Kong Cheuk Kwan* v *R* (1985).

However, there has been a return to gross negligence as a type of manslaughter in *R* v *Adomako* (1995), where the question was said to be: '...having regard to the risk of death, was the defendant's conduct in the circumstances so bad as to amount to a criminal act or omission...?' There are a further three questions to ask:
- Did the defendant owe the victim a duty of care?
- Did a breach of this duty cause the death?
- If the answer to both the above is yes, was the act or omission amounting to the breach of duty so negligent as to go beyond mere compensation and amount to a crime?

The courts have accepted many situations in which a duty is owed including:
- the duty of a doctor to a patient (*R* v *Adomako*, 1995)
- the duty of a landlord to a tenant to keep the premises safe (*R* v *Singh*, 1998)
- a duty arising under a contract where there is an obligation to act (*R* v *Pittwood*, 1902)
- a duty where the defendant assumes responsibility for the care of another (*R* v *Stone and Dobinson*, 1977)
- a duty owed by a lorry driver for the safety of illegal immigrants who he knew were hidden in his lorry (*R* v *Wacker*, 2002)

Gross negligence manslaughter has been criticised for the circularity of the tests involved and also for the use of civil terminology.

Reckless manslaughter

Reckless manslaughter based on the Cunningham model was traditionally available wherever the defendant was aware of a risk and nevertheless carried on to take it, and the taking of the risk resulted in death (*R* v *Pike*, 1961).

The application of subjective recklessness was denied in both *R* v *Seymour* (1983) and *R* v *Lawrence* (1982) at a time when Caldwell objective recklessness was preferred. Prior to *R* v *Adomako* (1995), the law did recognise the possibility of objective recklessness in relation to a charge of manslaughter. In *Adomako* this was held to be wrong, since recklessness should mean that the defendant had been indifferent to the risk of injury, or had foreseen the risk but nevertheless carried on and taken it.

In *R* v *Lidar* (2000), subjective recklessness appears to have been reintroduced. The case actually concerned an appeal on sentencing. However, the judge, responding to the complaint that the jury had not been directed on gross negligence, identified that this was unnecessary where recklessness was an issue.

Reform of involuntary manslaughter

The Law Commission Report on Involuntary Manslaughter (No 237) in 1996 identified a number of problems with the law on manslaughter:

- the uncertainty of the circumstances in which an omission can lead to liability
- the breadth of the offence which causes difficulties in applying sentences
- the devaluing effect that this can have on more serious examples of the crime
- the fact that manslaughter is 'unprincipled because it requires only that a foreseeable risk of causing some harm' is needed when the defendant is actually convicted of causing death
- the problems associated with the objective character of gross negligence

As a result, the Law Commission has suggested two draft offences:
- **Reckless killing:** where the defendant is aware of a risk that his or her conduct will cause death or serious injury and it is unreasonable for him or her to take that risk in all the circumstances.
- **Gross carelessness killing:** where the risk that the defendant's conduct will cause death/serious injury is obvious to a reasonable person in his or her position, and the defendant is capable of appreciating that risk at all material times. Either his or her conduct falls well below what can reasonably be expected in the circumstances, or the defendant intends by his or her conduct to cause some injury, or is aware of, and unreasonably takes, the risk that it may do so.

General defences

It is necessary to make a distinction between those defences which, in effect, claim a lack of criminal capacity by the defendant, and those which are claimed as either a justification or as an excuse for the offence in question.

The first type of defence implies that when the offence occurred, the defendant was incapable of forming the necessary criminal intent, of making a rational judgement or of completing a voluntary act. The second type usually implies that the defendant was still capable of exercising a rational judgement but may have been justified in committing the crime, e.g. doing so in self-defence, and therefore he or she should escape conviction and be excused, as in the case of duress.

Defences can operate in different ways. They may:
- involve the prosecution failing to make out one or more elements of the crime. For example, there is no *actus reus* in non-insane automatism because the act is not voluntary.
- place an evidential burden on the defendant. For example, in the case of necessity the defendant would need to explain why it was necessary to carry out the act.
- place a legal burden on the defendant. For example, a defendant claiming insanity as a defence would need to prove each aspect of the M'Naghten test for legal insanity.
- be complete defences and have the effect of relieving the defendant of liability altogether, while insanity, for instance, may still result in incarceration in an institution.

- be available for all crimes but others may or may not apply to specific crimes. For example, duress is not available for murder, attempted murder and secondary participation in murder.

The defences listed here should not be confused with the three precise defences that are found in the **Homicide Act 1957**. Those defences are special and partial defences and operate only in respect of a murder charge, reducing it to one of manslaughter.

Insanity

Insanity can be pleaded in relation to all offences except those of strict liability (in strict liability offences there is no requirement of *mens rea*). Where a plea of insanity is accepted, the defendant may claim not to be responsible for the commission of the offence, and therefore is not guilty by reason of insanity.

A plea of insanity has become rare in modern times because:
- since the **Homicide Act 1957**, a plea of diminished responsibility has been available in answer to a charge of murder
- in 1965, the death penalty was abolished, meaning there is now a less pressing need to prove such a plea
- before the **Criminal Procedure (Insanity and Unfitness to Plead) Act 1991** it could mean an indefinite stay in a mental institution; now this only definitely happens where the charge is murder, and there are a number of possible orders currently available to a judge, including an order for admission to hospital with or without a restriction order, a guardianship order, a supervision and treatment order or an absolute discharge

According to the M'Naghten rules, which originated from *R* v *M'Naghten* (1843), to establish a defence on the grounds of insanity it must be clearly proved that at the time of committing the act:

> ...the party accused was labouring under such a defect of reason, from disease of the mind, as not to know the nature and quality of the act he was doing; or, if he did know it, that he did not know that what he was doing was wrong.

Juries are told that everybody is to be presumed sane, and therefore responsible for their actions, unless the contrary is proved. The defendant has the legal burden of proving insanity on a balance of probabilities, although the prosecution might raise insanity, for example to rebut a defence claim of automatism.

There are three essential elements to this defence: (1) a defect of reason; (2) caused by a disease of the mind; and (3) the defendant as a result either did not know the nature or quality of his/her act, or, if he/she did, then he/she did not know that it was wrong.

Disease of the mind

In this context, 'disease of the mind' is a legal term and not a medical term. Disease of the mind does not have to refer purely to mental diseases. It could, for instance, refer to a physical disease, provided that it is one that affects the mind, as was accepted in the case of epilepsy in *R* v *Sullivan* (1983), the hyperglycaemia associated with diabetes in *R* v *Hennessy* (1989) and indeed the arteriosclerosis in *R* v *Kemp* (1957), which affected the flow of blood to the brain.

Disease of the mind is identified as an internal factor. External factors cannot be dealt with under the defence of insanity, although they might be appropriate to non-insane automatism. The effects of diabetes are a good way of demonstrating the distinction. A person suffering from diabetes may develop hyperglycaemia, where there is too much glucose circulating in the blood, which can then lead to trances, coma and ultimately death. Diabetics may need to inject themselves with insulin in order to suppress the effects of high blood-sugar levels. As in *Hennessy*, a person who has forgotten to take insulin and then commits a crime while in a hyperglycaemic state can be said to be suffering from a disease of the mind, since it is an internal factor. On the other hand, diabetics who inject with insulin need to eat regularly to maintain reasonable blood-sugar levels or they may suffer hypoglycaemia (low blood-sugar levels), which can also lead to trances and a coma. A person who commits a crime while suffering hypoglycaemia would not be able to claim insanity since the state is induced by an external factor, namely the failure to eat, as was identified in *R* v *Quick* (1973). Non-insane automatism may provide a defence in such circumstances.

Disease of the mind could, however, include mental illnesses that are reoccurring and that lead to criminal activity. This can be seen in *R* v *Burgess* (1991), where the defendant had been sleepwalking and wounded a neighbour, and the delusional state in *M'Naghten*.

Defect of reason

This means that the disease of the mind must have impaired the defendant's powers of reasoning. It would therefore be impossible to claim insanity where the defendant is merely suffering from confusion or absent-mindedness (*R* v *Clarke*, 1972).

'...did not know the nature or quality of his act or that the act was wrong'

The defendant may or may not be aware of what he/she is doing because of impaired consciousness and therefore he/she may or may not be aware that it was wrong. 'Did not know that his act was wrong' means that the defendant was unaware that the act was 'legally' wrong rather than not knowing that it was 'morally' wrong. Thus the defendant in *R* v *Windle* (1952) could not claim insanity because he commented that he expected that he might be hanged for the killing. Similarly, in *R* v *Johnson* (2007) a paranoid schizophrenic suffering from delusions was denied the defence because psychiatrists accepted that he knew his acts were legally wrong even if he believed that he was not morally wrong.

The M'Naghten rules have been much criticised because they:

- are based on a legal definition made at a point in history when there was little real knowledge or understanding of mental illness
- are generally incompatible with psychiatric reasoning since the definition is legal rather than medical
- can lead to absurd distinctions as in *Hennessy* and *Quick*, and do not reflect real responsibility
- protect some people who are clearly not insane in a medical sense, such as epileptics, but not others whom we might easily think are medically insane, such as Byrne and his 'uncontrollable impulses' (*R* v *Byrne*, 1960)

Reforms have been suggested, for example by the Butler Committee on Mentally Abnormal Offenders in 1975, which wanted to replace the defence of insanity with one of 'not guilty by reason of mental disorder'. There is also an extensive provision in the Draft Criminal Code. Under Clause 35 of the Code, such a verdict of 'not guilty by reason of mental disorder' can be returned when it is shown on a balance of probabilities (by defence or prosecution) that the defendant was suffering from severe mental illness or severe mental handicap. Both of these terms are defined in Clause 34. Mental illness includes lasting impairment of intellectual functions, lasting alteration of mood, delusions, abnormal perception and disordered thinking so as to prevent proper communication. Mental handicap is described as a state of arrested or incomplete development of mind, which includes severe impairment of intelligence and social functioning. It is also possible for the prosecution to show (beyond reasonable doubt) that the offence was not attributable to the severe mental illness or handicap, in order to rebut the defence. Clause 36 provides a separate qualified defence, where it is accepted that the defendant is 'not guilty on evidence of mental disorder', which only applies to those offenders whose *mens rea* is affected by the disorder. (Clause 35 applies regardless of whether the disorder negates *mens rea*.) Therefore, Clause 36 covers the first limb of the M'Naghten rules — the defendant had no idea what he was doing; Clause 35 covers the second limb — the defendant knows the quality of his act but does not know it is wrong.

Non-insane automatism

The basic definition of automatism is found in Lord Denning's judgement in *Bratty* v *Attorney General for Northern Ireland* (1963):

> No act is punishable if it is done involuntarily; and an involuntary act in this context — some people nowadays prefer to speak of it as 'automatism' — means an act which is done by the muscles without any control by the mind, such as a spasm, a reflex action or convulsion; or an act done by a person who is not conscious of what he is doing, such as an act done whilst suffering from concussion or whilst sleepwalking...

Lawton CJ in *R* v *Quick* (1973) referred to the defence as '...a quagmire of law seldom entered into nowadays save by those in desperate need of a defence...'

Non-insane automatism is a narrow defence, since any kind of automatism that conforms to the M'Naghten rules will be classed as insanity and will lead to a verdict of 'not guilty by reason of insanity'. On the other hand, non-insane automatism will lead to an acquittal because the defendant's act is involuntary so there is no *actus reus*. The defence cannot be seen simply as a negation of *mens rea* because it is also available in the case of strict liability offences. There must be an external factor involved for non-insane automatism to succeed (*Hill* v *Baxter*, 1958).

The defence of non-insane automatism operates when the defendant acts in a state of unconsciousness or impaired consciousness such as concussion, so that his/her actions are involuntary (*Bratty* v *Attorney General for Northern Ireland*, 1963). It will not be accepted merely because the defendant's mind is acting imperfectly (*R* v *Isitt*, 1978). It will only operate when there is no voluntary act and the defendant's ability to control his/her actions is destroyed (*A-G's Reference (No. 2 of 1992)*, 1993).

Non-insane automatism cannot be a defence if the state of mind is self-induced in crimes of basic intent, but it may be used in the case of crimes of specific intent (*Bailey*, 1983 and *Quick*, 1973). Somnambulism (sleepwalking) was originally cited specifically by Lord Denning in *Bratty* and this was accepted in *R* v *Lillenfield* (1985). However, it has now been identified as an internal factor, appropriate only to insanity (*Burgess*, 1991).

Duress

Duress is a complete defence where the defendant accepts that all of the elements of the crime can be shown, but claims that he has an 'excuse' for committing the crime, and therefore should escape conviction. In duress, the burden of proof is on the prosecution to disprove, once the defendant has raised it as an issue, but the evidential burden is on the defendant to show that his/her mind was affected by the duress.

Duress of threats

The defendant has both *actus reus* and *mens rea* for the crime but conviction is escaped because his/her will is overborne by personal threats or by threats to family members. The defence operates differently from automatism, where the act is involuntary because the defendant, in effect, lacks conscious will. Here, the act may not be voluntary and so is mitigated, but it is conscious (*DPP for Northern Ireland* v *Lynch*, 1975).

For duress of threats to succeed, the jury will need to consider the two key questions raised by Lord Lane CJ in *Graham* (1982):

- Was the defendant impelled to act by real fear of threat of death or injury to self or family?
- If so, would a sober person of reasonable firmness sharing the characteristics of the defendant have acted in the same way?

The first question concerns the type of threat that is sufficient for the defence to apply. Threats of death or serious physical violence may be sufficient (*R* v *Howe*, 1987), and the threat need not be to the defendant but can be to his/her family members (*R* v *K*, 1984 and *R* v *Ortiz*, 1986). It is unlikely that other threats will suffice (*R* v *Valderrama-Vega*, 1985), particularly threats to property. This can seem unfair since, if the defendant's will is overborne, it is inconsistent if the defence lacks universal application.

The second question concerns the gravity of the threat, and the defendant must show that a person of reasonable firmness would have acted in the same way (*DPP* v *Jones*, 1990 and *R* v *Bowen*, 1996).

To be successful, the defendant must show a connection between the threat and his/her act, so there must be a threat aimed at making the defendant commit a specific offence (*R* v *Cole*, 1994).

The defence is not available where the defendant has voluntarily associated with those who are likely to subject him/her to duress (*R* v *Sharp*, 1987), although the defendant must have been aware of the violent tendencies of these associates before he/she will lose the defence (*R* v *Shepherd*, 1987). Prior awareness of the exact criminal activity that those exercising the duress might accept as an alternative to carrying out the threat is irrelevant; it is the awareness of the risk of compulsion that counts (*R* v *Heath*, 1999). However, if the defendant willingly associates with people whom he/she ought to realise would put him/her under pressure, then the defence will be unavailable (*R* v *Hasan*, 2005).

Duress is also unavailable where the defendant could avoid the effects of the threats (*R* v *Hudson and Taylor*, 1971), so the defence only succeeds where the defendant has no safe means of escape (*R* v *Gill*, 1963). However, the threats do not need to be carried out immediately, as long as they are imminent (*R* v *Abdul-Hussain*, 1999). The defendant must have a reasonable belief that the threats will definitely be carried out and are immediate or almost immediate (*R* v *Hasan*).

The defence is also not available for certain offences, including murder (*Abbot* v *R*, 1977), being an accessory to murder (*Howe*, 1987 overruling *Lynch*), and this has been applied even to a 13-year-old defendant (*R* v *Wilson*, 2007), attempted murder (*R* v *Gotts*, 1992) (this is particularly anomalous because it is available to s.18), and treason (Lord Goddard in *R* v *Steane*, 1947).

The defence was described in *Howe* as a 'concession to human frailty' — an acknowledgement that a person would generally put his/her own safety first. However, these limitations on the defence lead to obvious criticisms:
- There may be circumstances where even a person of reasonable fortitude would submit to threats and kill as a consequence.
- A person is, in effect, being forced to be a hero by the law.
- Alternatively, it could unnaturally force a person to allow his/her family to be harmed.
- Only a mandatory life sentence is available for murder, so there is no opportunity to use the defence as mitigation.

- It is argued that provocation excuses killing, so it is inconsistent and unfair that duress cannot.
- If duress is an excuse for a crime based on self-preservation then it ought to be fairly and consistently applied.
- In any case, self-defence is universally available.

The Law Commission has suggested reforms, including making the defence available for all offences.

Duress of circumstances

Duress of circumstances developed out of the unavailability of the defence of necessity and the limitations of the defence of duress of threats. Its origins were in those situations where the defendant was forced to act because of the circumstances rather than by any direct threats (*R* v *Willer*, 1987).

It was first identified as an available defence (and probably as a form of necessity) in *R* v *Conway* (1989). The defence has since been limited in application to where there is a fear of death or serious injury and a person of reasonable firmness would have reacted as the defendant did (*R* v *Martin*, 1989). Therefore, the two-part test from *R* v *Graham* (1982) must be applied. The defence will not be available where, on an objective examination, there is no imminent threat of harm (*Abdul-Hussain*, 1999). The defendant must reasonably believe that a threat existed, although there need not have been a real threat (*R* v *Safi*, 2003). In *R* v *Pommell* (1995), it was identified that the defence can apply to all crimes but, in line with duress of threats, it is not available for murder and attempted murder. Most cases have involved motoring offences.

In *Conway* (1989) and in the Court of Appeal in *R* v *Shayler* (2001), it was suggested that duress of circumstances is indistinguishable from the defence of necessity. However, the case of *Re A (Conjoined Twins)* (2000) would suggest otherwise, since necessity was accepted in that case as being available as a defence to murder if certain criteria were met.

The defence of duress of circumstances has been codified in the Draft Criminal Code.

Necessity

Necessity operates in a similar way to duress but it acts as a justification rather than an excuse — the defendant claims that he/she acted in order to avoid a greater evil. In duress, the source of the coercion is individuals, whereas in necessity it is natural forces.

Traditionally, the defence was generally considered not to be available (*R* v *Dudley and Stephens*, 1884), although this is not absolutely certain because of the lack of clarity and precision in Lord Coleridge's judgement. This general view of the defence, in any case, can clearly lead to injustice (*R* v *Kitson*, 1955) and there are obvious situations where the defence should apply. Situations where necessity was rejected have subsequently been covered by statutory provisions — for example, a rejection of the defence where emergency vehicles drive through red traffic lights (*Buckoke* v *GLC*, 1975). The defence has also been rejected as a justification for possession of cannabis as a means of pain relief (*R* v *Altham*, 2006).

The defence has been accepted on some limited and isolated occasions — for example, for the preservation of a woman's life in abortion (*R* v *Bourne*, 1939) and in certain clinical judgements (*Gillick* v *West Norfolk and Wisbech AHA*, 1986).

The modern law is contained in *Re A (Conjoined Twins)* (2000). Here, the Court of Appeal accepted that, in the circumstances, the defence could be used because the act for which necessity was claimed was carried out to avoid consequences that could not be avoided otherwise. Brooke LJ identified three necessary requirements for the defence to apply:
- The act was necessary to avoid an inevitable and irreparable evil.
- Nothing more was done than was reasonably necessary for the purpose to be achieved.
- The evil inflicted was not disproportionate to the evil avoided.

Re A is, of course, a civil case and therefore has only persuasive authority in criminal cases.

Intoxication

Intoxication, if successful, is another defence that is based on the incapacitation of the defendant. As a defence, it applies to drugs as well as to alcohol (*R* v *Hardie*, 1984) and also to substances, e.g. glue sniffing. The rules on using intoxication as a defence tend to reflect society's general dislike of intoxication or any excessive behaviour (*DPP* v *Majewski*, 1977). The dilemma of how to deal with a 'drunken' offender is compounded because so many offences are committed while in an intoxicated state. Certainly, intoxication will never be available as a defence if used purely as 'Dutch courage' (*Attorney General for Northern Ireland* v *Gallagher*, 1963).

Intoxication does not act as an excuse but it may either:
- prevent the defendant from forming the *mens rea* for the crime, or
- cause the defendant to act under a mistake

The law draws a distinction between crimes of specific intent and crimes of basic intent when considering intoxication as a defence. It does so because recklessness is available as the mental element in basic intent crimes, and voluntary intoxication can be reckless in itself. Therefore intoxication, if voluntary, may provide no defence in basic intent crimes because it is, in fact, proof of the *mens rea* (*Majewski*, 1977). In general, self-induced intoxication is not available as a defence where recklessness is sufficient *mens rea* (*Caldwell*, 1982), and the courts usually take the view that a mistake induced by intoxication is a reckless mistake (*R* v *Woods*, 1982 and *R* v *O'Grady*, 1987).

However, voluntary intoxication may be a defence to crimes of specific intent because the *mens rea* may be negated, and this is justified because it is possible sometimes for an alternative crime to be accepted (*DPP* v *Beard*, 1920).

Sometimes the result of pleading the defence can be complicated by the statute creating the offence making the defence appear to be wider, as in the **Criminal Damage Act 1971** s.5: 'If at the time of the act...he believed that the person or persons whom he believed to be entitled to consent to the destruction or damage...had so consented or would have so consented...' (*Jaggard* v *Dickinson*, 1981).

Involuntary intoxication could occur in one of three ways:
- a spiked drink — in this case, the fact that there is no blame does not negate *mens rea*, so there can still be a conviction (*R* v *Kingston*, 1995), although in some circumstances it might alter the way in which the defendant is treated (*R* v *Shippam*, 1971)
- prescribed drugs — here the defence may negate *mens rea*, but it would still result in conviction if the defendant knew the consequences of taking the drugs
- unpredictable reactions to drugs — here the result may depend on whether taking them is reckless or not (*Hardie*, 1984)

Generally a mistake caused through intoxication will not be available as a defence (*O'Grady*), and the same also applies where intoxication results in mistaken identity (*R* v *Fotheringham*, 1988). However, a slightly different line was taken in *R* v *Richardson and Irwin* (1999). A drunken mistake about the amount of force required in self-defence is also not a defence.

Non-fatal offences against the person

Assaults

Traditionally, assault and battery were common-law offences, which are now found as separate summary offences in s.39 of the **Criminal Justice Act 1988**. Section 40 clouds the issue by referring to 'common assault' only, but the Court of Appeal has resolved the issue by taking a wide view and treating this as a generic term (*R* v *Lynsey*, 1995). The offences have been described as statutory (*DPP* v *Little*, 1992) but there are no statutory definitions, so these must be found in the common law. Many of the same difficulties exist in criminal law concerning assault and battery as they do in tort law, in respect of what the difference is between the two, and how broad or narrow the concept of assault should be framed.

The other three more serious offences are defined in the **Offences Against the Person Act 1861**.

Assault

This is defined as 'the intentional or reckless causing of an apprehension of immediate unlawful personal violence' (*R* v *Venna*, 1976).

The *actus reus* for assault is:
* doing an act that causes the other person to apprehend immediate violence; however, the assault must involve either an act or threatening words — an omission is not sufficient for assault (*Fagan* v *Metropolitan Police Commissioner*, 1969)

The *mens rea* for assault is:
* the intention to cause the apprehension, or
* recklessness as to whether the apprehension is caused; Cunningham subjective recklessness is the appropriate test (*R* v *Spratt*, 1991, *DPP* v *Parmenter*, 1991 and *R* v *Savage*, 1991)

The victim need not be put in fear but merely made aware that violence is imminent (*Smith* v *Superintendent of Woking Police Station*, 1983) and the victim may be put in fear even though the violence is unlikely, so an assault can be committed where there is no contact. In fact, there can be an assault even where the defendant did not actually intend to carry out the battery.

Traditionally, it was doubted that words alone would be sufficient to amount to an assault, though they might negate one (*Tuberville* v *Savage*, 1669). However, where accompanied by gestures, words can be part of assault (*Read* v *Coker*, 1853), particularly where weapons are involved (*R* v *Wilson*, 1955). More recently, 'silence' has been accepted as sufficient to amount to an assault (*R* v *Ireland*, 1996). This was based on the principle (approved in *R* v *Chan-Fook*, 1994, since upheld by the House of Lords) that 'actual bodily harm' could include psychiatric injury. This means that technically *Ireland* should be battery rather than assault (and the case has been criticised by Professor J. C. Smith on this basis).

Battery

This has been defined variously as:
* 'the least touching of someone in anger' (*Cole* v *Turner*, 1705)
* 'the actual intended use of unlawful force to another person without his consent' (*Fagan* v *Metropolitan Police Commissioner*, 1969)
* 'the actual infliction of unlawful force on another person' (*Collins* v *Wilcox*, 1984)
* 'any intentional touching without the consent of that person and without lawful excuse. It need not be hostile or rude or aggressive as some cases seem to indicate' (*Faulkner* v *Talbot*, 1981 per Lord Lane on indecent assault)

The *actus reus* of battery is:
* the inflicting of unlawful force upon another

The *mens rea* of battery is:
* the intention to inflict the unlawful force, or
* recklessness as to whether the unlawful force is inflicted

Therefore, battery must involve the physical application of some kind of unlawful force, although it appears that the force does not always have to be directly applied (*DPP* v *K*, 1990), and it may not always require a direct touching (*Thomas*, 1985). It also appears that battery can be committed by an omission when there is a duty to act — for example, a failure to warn of the presence of a hypodermic syringe during a search of pockets was considered battery in *DPP* v *Santana-Bermudez* (2003).

It is possible that battery could involve a continuing act (*R* v *Fagan MPC*, 1969). While it has been said that it must involve 'hostility' (*Wilson* v *Pringle*, 1987), other cases have cast doubt on this view (*F* v *West Berkshire Health Authority*, 1990).

There is some doubt whether the battery must be 'intentional'; if so, it would be more difficult to prove than the more serious offence of malicious wounding under s.20 of the **Offences Against the Person Act 1861**.

Both assault and battery are basic intent crimes for the purpose of using intoxication as a defence, which is therefore impossible, as either may be proved by recklessness.

Reform

There have been recommendations for reform of the area of assault, which are found in Clause 6 of Law Commission Report No. 218. This suggests an offence stated as following:

(1) A person is guilty of the offence of assault if:
  (a) he intentionally or recklessly applies force to or causes an impact on the body of another
    (i) without the consent of the other; or
    (ii) where the act is intended or likely to cause injury, with or without the consent of the other, or
  (b) he intentionally or recklessly, without the consent of the other, causes the other to believe that any such force or impact is imminent
(2) No such offence is committed if the force or impact, not being intended or likely to cause injury, is in the circumstances such as is generally acceptable in the ordinary conduct of daily life and the defendant does not know or believe that it is in fact unacceptable to the other person.

One major effect of this would be to remove battery as a separate offence. Clause 75 of the Draft Criminal Code is a simplified version of the above.

Section 47 of the Offences Against the Person Act 1861: assault occasioning actual bodily harm

Assault occasioning actual bodily harm is a statutory offence found in s.47 of the **Offences Against the Person Act 1861** and the least serious of those offences contained in the Act. In essence, it is a common assault that includes an aggravating factor — the actual bodily harm.

The *actus reus* of this offence is assault or battery or both, which results in 'actual bodily harm'. The *mens rea* is intending the assault/battery, or recklessness.

Unlike common assault, this offence is triable either way. One strange feature of the offence is that it carries the same maximum sentence as for an s.20 offence (5 years' imprisonment), even though the two offences are supposed to represent different levels of seriousness. In practice, a lesser sentence will always be given for s.47 in comparison to s.20.

There is no definition of 'actual bodily harm' in the **Offences Against the Person Act** but it clearly involves something less than serious harm. It has been defined as including 'any hurt or injury calculated (which probably means "likely") to interfere with the health or comfort of the victim' (*R v Miller*, 1954). It has also been held to mean 'not so trivial as to be wholly insignificant' (*Chan-Fook*, 1994). However, it can include psychiatric injury (*Ireland*, 1997) and will represent some actual harm varying between trivial and serious. For example:

- four or five bruises caused by a belt (*R v Smith*, 1985)
- minor abrasions and a bruise (*R v Jones*, 1981)
- a painful kick to the stomach leaving some tenderness though no visible injury (*Reigate JJ ex p Counsell*, 1983)
- a momentary loss of consciousness (*R(T) v DPP*, 2003)
- cutting off a pony tail (*DPP v Smith*, 2006)

The necessary *mens rea* is, in effect, the same as for common-law assault — intention, or recklessness (*R v Roberts*, 1971). Recklessness means that an indirect cause is possible, as long as the victim's actions do not break the chain of causation. The type of recklessness appropriate is Cunningham recklessness measured subjectively (*Spratt*, 1991). In *Spratt* it was stated that the defendant must intentionally or recklessly occasion actual bodily harm, while the case of *Savage* suggests that intentional or reckless battery is sufficient. The House of Lords in *Savage* held that the issue of occasioning actual bodily harm is purely an issue of causation, so all that the prosecution has to prove is that the defendant intentionally or recklessly assaulted the victim and that actual bodily harm then resulted.

Wounding and grievous bodily harm

In theory, there is a 'hierarchy' of wounding offences, ranked in order of seriousness. However, there are a number of complications. For example:

- The language used makes it difficult to distinguish the *actus reus* of the different wounding offences — the words 'unlawful' and 'malicious' occur in both.
- The language used in the 1861 Act is confusing and archaic — for example, what is the difference between 'causing' and 'inflicting'?
- It is hard to say what an effective hierarchy of offences should be based on — the seriousness of the harm caused or the seriousness of the harm intended?
- The defences, particularly consent, can provide added complications. (See section on consent, pp. 47–48.)

It is not surprising, therefore, that the area has been subject to calls for major reform. As the Law Commission stated in Report 218:

> The interests both of justice and social protection would be much better served by a law that was:
> (i) clearly and briefly stated;
> (ii) based on the injury intended or contemplated by the accused, and not on what he happened to cause; and
> (iii) governed by clear distinctions, expressed in modern and comprehensible language between serious and less serious cases

Within the 1861 Act, there are two offences that relate to wounding and grievous bodily harm, and by definition these are the more serious non-fatal offences. Not surprisingly, they are themselves ranked in order of seriousness, and a different sentencing regime applies to the two. S.18 carries a maximum sentence of life imprisonment, whereas s.20 carries a maximum sentence of 5 years.

It is worth remembering that the legislature in 1861 was consolidating existing law rather than preparing a codified criminal statute. This may partly explain the confusions that the statutory definitions create, such as:

- There are two ways of committing both wounding and grievous bodily harm.
- S.18 differs from s.20 in requiring an ulterior intent.
- The word 'malice' is applied to both offences but does not equate with the meaning of malice when in connection with murder, and has a different application in either offence.
- The word used for the active part of each offence of GBH differs between the two offences — 'cause' in s.18 and 'inflict' in s.20.

As a result, there have been constant calls for reform in this area.

Section 20 of the Offences Against the Person Act 1861

Under s.20: 'Whosoever shall unlawfully and maliciously wound or inflict any grievous bodily harm upon any other person, either with or without any weapon or instrument, shall be guilty of an offence...'

The *actus reus* of this offence is:
- unlawfully wounding, or
- unlawfully inflicting grievous bodily harm

The *mens rea* of the offence is malice, simply meaning intention or recklessness.

Wounding and GBH are both defined in the same way as in s.18. There are still a number of problems concerning s.20, however. The major problem concerns the word 'inflict'. The original problem created by this word was whether or not it required a direct assault or whether, like 'cause' in s.18, an indirect action amounted to an infliction. For example, in *R v Martin* (1881), the action created a panic in which people were injured. This was considered to be an infliction, so s.20 was available. However, in *R v Clarence* (1888), where withholding of information led to an infection (the wife contracting gonorrhoea), it was held on appeal to be too indirect to amount to an infliction. It has since been suggested that there can be an 'infliction' without fear and therefore without an assault.

Ireland (1997) and *R* v *Burstow* (1997) have moved the law on to recognition that psychiatric injury can be used as a basis for both assault and wounding. *Burstow* accepted that psychiatric injury can be 'inflicted' and so a charge under s.20 ought to be pursued. This case is also interesting for examining the difference between 'cause' and 'inflict'. While *R* v *Mandair* (1994) recognises that 'cause' must necessarily include 'inflict' for the purposes of accepting convictions on the lesser charge, the Court of Appeal in *Burstow* considered that it would be undesirable to maintain that there was a practical difference between the two words — the significant difference then being the available sentence.

The *mens rea* has proved equally problematic. 'Malicious' is generally accepted as meaning reckless in s.20. The appropriate measure of recklessness is the Cunningham subjective type. In *R* v *Mowatt* (1968) it was held that the defendant must foresee some harm, e.g. some battery, but not necessarily the gravity of the harm inflicted. Glanville Williams has argued that this is wrong and that the defendant should foresee the actual risk in order to be liable under s.20. This was the stance taken in *R* v *Sullivan* (1981), but was then clouded by a more objective Caldwell approach taken in *DPP* v *K* (1990). However, the appropriate measure is now that identified in *Spratt*, *Parmenter* and *Savage*.

Section 18 of the Offences Against the Person Act 1861

Under s.18:

> Whosoever shall unlawfully and maliciously by any means whatsoever wound or cause any grievous bodily harm to any person with intent to do some grievous bodily harm to some person or with intent to resist or prevent the lawful apprehension or detainer of any person shall be guilty of an offence.

The *actus reus* of the offence is:
- to unlawfully wound, or
- to cause grievous bodily harm

The *mens rea* is:
- intending to cause GBH or to resist or prevent lawful apprehension, or
- intentionally or recklessly wounding with intent to cause GBH or to resist or prevent lawful apprehension

Therefore, if wounding with intent were charged, then 'malicious' is irrelevant because only ulterior intent is sufficient *mens rea*. However, if malicious wounding is charged, then malice can refer to the wounding that is being carried out, intentionally or recklessly.

The first aspect of the *actus reus* requiring definition is the meaning of 'to wound'. This must involve piercing of both the dermis and the epidermis, i.e. the top layer and deeper layers of the skin (*JCC* v *Eisenhower*, 1984), so a scratch may not suffice, and even if it produces blood and bruising, however severe, it will not be considered as wounding.

The next aspect requiring definition is 'grievous bodily harm'. This has been defined as 'really serious harm' in *DPP* v *Smith* (1961). However, it is unlikely that 'really' is a vital element and the harm probably does not have to be life endangering (*Bullerton*, 1992). It is also possible that psychiatric harm may suffice (*Ireland*, 1997 and *Burstow*, 1997).

Another major issue of the *actus reus* is causation. 'Cause' has a wider application than 'inflict' in s.20. Generally, a result can be 'caused' by indirect means where something can only be 'inflicted' directly by the application of force. In s.18, general principles of causation apply, so that the defendant can 'cause' the result by his/her omission to act when a duty to act is owed. Cause in s.18 could also include, for example, poisoning, where neither battery nor the application of force is involved. This is clearly an anomaly, since it results in the fact that on the issue of causation, the more serious s.18 offence is easier to prove than the s.20 offence.

Since different words are used in the offences, it has posed difficulties in showing that the more serious non-fatal offences incorporate the less serious, so that a verdict could be brought on the lesser charge (*Mandair*, 1994). It is also possible that a person charged with attempted murder could be convicted by the jury of s.18 instead (*R* v *Mitchell*, 2003).

The first significant point regarding the *mens rea* is that it requires ulterior intent, so there are two aspects to it:
- malice (meaning intent or recklessness), and
- the intent either to cause grievous bodily harm, or to resist or prevent arrest

Intent has the same meaning as in murder, so it is specific intent measured by desire of consequences or foresight of consequences, according to the established test. Recklessness is measured subjectively according to the Cunningham test (*R* v *Morrison*, 1989 and *R* v *Farrell*, 1989).

The requirement of ulterior intent and the fact that the offence can occur in a combination of ways presents a number of apparent inconsistencies:
- Where the defendant causes GBH with intent to cause GBH, the word 'malicious' has been held to be superfluous and it is impossible to recklessly intend (*Mowatt*, 1968).
- If the defendant is charged with malicious wounding with intent to cause GBH, it is possible for the defendant to be reckless as to the wounding while having intent to commit the GBH.
- If the defendant is charged with causing GBH with intent to resist arrest, 'malicious' is clearly not superfluous, since otherwise the defendant would be guilty without any foresight of harm resulting.

Perhaps it is not surprising that the ex-chairman of the Law Commission referred to the 'chaotic structure of the law of offences against the person'.

Reform of wounding and GBH offences

Simple reforms suggested by the Law Commission include the adoption of three new offences:

- intentionally causing serious harm — carrying a maximum sentence of life imprisonment
- recklessly causing serious harm — carrying a maximum sentence of 5 years' imprisonment
- intentionally or recklessly causing injury

The appropriate measure of recklessness would be the subjective Cunningham type. However, the definitions actually differ from the Draft Criminal Code, which refer to harm rather than injury.

Defences

Self-defence and prevention of crime

Self-defence has been available as part of the common law for a long time. It covers those actions that aim to prevent either injury to self or others, or loss or damage to property (*R* v *Cousins*, 1982). Prevention of crime is an associated defence but is statutory in character. It is covered by s.3 of the **Criminal Law Act 1967**: '...may use such force as is reasonable in circumstances in prevention of crime...or assisting in the lawful arrest of offenders...'. Both defences act as defences of justification, so a person has no duty in law to retreat but may stand and defend him/herself.

What amounts to reasonable force depends on the circumstances in which the defendant has to defend him/herself (*R* v *Whyte*, 1987). The defendant should be judged according to the facts as he/she saw them (*A-G's Reference (No. 2 of 1983)*, 1984). The court is unable to return a verdict of manslaughter rather than murder when excessive force is used ostensibly as self-defence (*R* v *Clegg*, 1995). In general, the measure of force necessary is objectively tested, but against circumstances as the defendant saw them. A defendant may claim that he or she mistakenly acted in self-defence (*R* v *Williams*, 1987) or was mistaken in the amount of force that was necessary in the circumstances, provided that the mistake is genuine.

Consent

One of the major problems of offences against the person is the extent to which consent can be used as a defence.

Consent can be either express or implied through custom, e.g. we impliedly consent to the 'ordinary brushes of life', such as being pushed against somebody on a tube train in the rush hour. It has been suggested, however, that implied consent can lead to grave difficulties when applied to the young or mentally disordered (Lord Goff in *Re F*, 1990). As a result, people who cannot understand the nature of the act they are consenting to, can generally not provide the defence of consent for the defendant (*Burrell* v *Harmer*, 1967). Consent is not generally removed by fraud or deception, except where the deception concerns the identity of the accused (*R* v *Clarence*, 1888) or the nature of the act (*R* v *Richardson*, 1998). However, both *Clarence* and *Richardson* were distinguished in *R* v *Tabassum* (2000), when the Court of Appeal drew a distinction between consent to the 'nature' of touching and consent 'as to its quality', so the context is also important. In *R* v *Bree* (2007) it was held that a drunken consent is still consent as long as the victim is not too drunk to make a choice.

There are, however, certain types of behaviour for which the law will not allow the defence of consent. For example:

- prize fighting (*R* v *Coney*, 1882) (though more severe injuries may be sustained quite lawfully in boxing under proper rules)
- sadomasochistic activities for sexual pleasure (*R* v *Brown*, 1994); this tends to reiterate the position in *R* v *Donovan* (1934) on inflicting harm for sexual purposes; more recently it has been suggested that changing social attitudes to injury during sexual activities should be considered (*R* v *Boyea*, 1992)
- ritual mutilation; this is generally considered unlawful and beyond consent, e.g. the **Prohibition of Female Circumcision Act 1985**, although it would appear that some level of disfigurement can be consented to, most notably where it falls within marriage (*R* v *Wilson*, 1996)
- transmission of a sexual disease (*R* v *Dica*, 2003)

While consent to childish 'horseplay' has been accepted for some time (*R* v *Jones*, 1986) this principle has also been extended to adult horseplay (*R* v *Aitken*, 1992).

The law on consent is in some confusion, and unsurprisingly, the Law Commission has suggested the following reforms:

- Consent should be available in the case of assaults that involve recklessly or intentionally applying force, but not to assault that is intended to cause injury or is likely to cause injury.
- If this is an unacceptable line, then the line should be drawn between injury and serious injury.

The dividing line is said to be what is in the public's interest. More recently the Court of Appeal has held that the line at which the issue of consent becomes immaterial is where there is a realistic risk of permanent harm (*R* v *Emmett*, 1999).

The two areas where consent will commonly be an issue are contact sports, providing that they are played within the legitimate rules, and medical treatment for the benefit of the patient.

Offences against property

Theft

Theft is defined in s.1(1) of the **Theft Act 1968**: 'A person is guilty of theft if he dishonestly appropriates property belonging to another with the intention of permanently depriving the other of it; and "thief" and "steal" shall be construed accordingly.' Sections 2–6 that follow are interpretation sections that give a detailed meaning of the various elements of the offence. Theft is (for obvious reasons) an offence that can be triable either way.

The *actus reus* of theft is:
- the appropriation
- of the property
- belonging to another

The *mens rea* is:
- dishonesty and
- the intention to permanently deprive

The separate elements of both the *actus reus* and the *mens rea* have created difficulties for interpretation, and each one must be considered carefully since each needs to be proved separately.

Appropriation

Appropriation is the active part of the *actus reus*. It was introduced in the **Theft Act 1968** as an alternative to the requirement under larceny that 'the thing should be carried away', with the hope that this terminology would be more easily understood.

Appropriation is defined in both a positive and a negative sense in s.3:
- Under s.3(1), 'any assumption by a person of the right of an owner amounts to an appropriation, and this includes, where he has come by the property (innocently or not) without stealing it, any later assumption of a right to it by keeping it or dealing with it as owner'.
- Under s.3(2), 'where property or a right or interest in property is or purports to be transferred for value to a person acting in good faith, no later assumption by him of rights which he believed himself to be acquiring shall, by reason of any defect in the transferor's title, amount to theft of the property'.

In *DPP* v *Gomez* (1993), Lord Lowry approved the dictionary meaning of appropriation as 'to take possession of, take to oneself, particularly without authority' and added that it meant 'to treat as one's own, property which belongs to someone else'. Therefore, appropriation is a much broader concept than mere 'taking' — for example, destruction could still be an appropriation. It is also sufficient that any of the rights of the owner are interfered with. It does not have to involve all of the owner's rights (*R* v *Morris*, 1983).

A major difficulty of 'appropriation' is the effect of the owner's consent. The previous law in the **Larceny Act 1916** required proof that the taking was without the owner's consent. However, s.3 is silent on this issue. The case law has proved contradictory. The original view was that of Lord Dilhorne in *R* v *Lawrence* (1971) that 'Parliament, by the omission of these words, has relieved the prosecution of the burden of establishing that the taking was without the owner's consent'. So here, taking possession of something was sufficient and there was no need for the 'appropriation' to interfere with the victim's rights at all. However, the reverse view was taken in *Morris* (1983) and before that in *Eddy* v *Niman* (1981), that the appropriation must involve some adverse interference with the rights of the owner, and the appropriation would occur at the point at which the unauthorised use of the property took place (*R* v *Skipp*, 1975).

There was therefore a division; *Morris* had contradicted *Lawrence* without overruling it. This has subsequently been settled in *Gomez* (1993), which approved *Lawrence* and disapproved *Morris*, so that consent is irrelevant (although Lord Lowry dissenting felt that this was ignoring the meaning intended in the Criminal Law Revision Committee 8th Report, which led to the **Theft Act 1968**, and that s.15 should be used for all offences involving deception).

Gomez has a number of key consequences:
- While possibly simplifying the law on appropriation it broadens the law on theft considerably.
- It makes appropriation a neutral term so that the emphasis is on the presence or absence of dishonesty.
- The appropriation can then occur at an earlier stage than it would have done in *Morris*, i.e. as soon as the goods are touched rather than at the point at which something is done that is inconsistent with the owner's rights.
- An almost total overlap between theft and obtaining property by deception is created.

Two subsequent cases have followed the principle in *Gomez* — one to prevent money being extracted by unscrupulous people from those of low intellect (*R* v *Hinks*, 2000), and the other to prevent charging elderly people excessive prices (*R* v *Williams*, 2000). In both cases, defence arguments focusing on civil property laws failed. However, there has also been subsequent inconsistent case law (*R* v *Gallasso*, 1993 and *R* v *Mazo*, 1996). Another problem is whether appropriation can be a continuous act, or whether property can be appropriated more than once. This seems to have been settled in the negative in *R* v *Atakpu* (1994). *R* v *Briggs* (2003) identifies that there is no appropriation where there is no physical act or where it is considered too remote.

Property

Defining property is important because this will determine what can and cannot be stolen. Property is at least partially defined in s.4(1): 'Property includes money and all other property, real or personal, including things in action and other intangible property.'

Section 4(1) is therefore potentially a very wide provision. It includes money (coins, bank notes and foreign money), as well as intangible things, such as debts and cheques (*R* v *Kohn*, 1979). Personal property, such as the paper on which a cheque is produced, could also come under the Act (*Oxford* v *Moss*, 1978).

However, other subsections of s.4 and decisions of the courts have limited the breadth of the general definition. According to s.4(2):

A person cannot steal land or things forming part of land and severed from it by him or by his direction except:

(a) when he is trustee or personal representative, or is authorised by power of attorney, or as a liquidator of a company, or otherwise, to sell or dispose of the land or anything forming part of it by dealing with it in breach of the confidence reposed in him; or

(b) when he is not in possession of the land and appropriates anything forming part of it by severing it or causing it to be severed, or after it has been severed; or

(c) when, being in possession of the land under a tenancy, he appropriates the whole or part of any fixture or structure let to be used with the land

So (a) could occur where a trustee sold a plot of land for his own purposes; (b) might occur where a farmer unlawfully allowed his cattle to graze on someone else's land; and (c) could occur where a tenant removed light fittings that were present in the premises when the lease commenced.

According to s.4(3):

A person who picks mushrooms growing wild on any land, or who picks flowers, fruit or foliage from a plant growing wild on any land, does not (although not in possession of the land), steal what he picks, unless he does it for reward or for sale or for other commercial purpose. For purposes of this subsection 'mushroom' includes any fungus, and 'plant' includes any shrub or tree.

Therefore the provision only affects those who take in order to profit.

According to s.4(4):

Wild creatures, tamed or untamed, shall be regarded as property; but a person cannot steal a wild creature not tamed nor ordinarily kept in captivity, or the carcase of any such creature, unless either it has been reduced into possession by or on behalf of another person and possession of it has not since been lost or abandoned, or another person is in course of reducing it into possession.

Confidential information is not property (*Oxford* v *Moss*, 1978). Similarly, electronically stored information is not property, but there are now offences under the **Computer Misuse Act 1990** concerning breaking into other people's computer systems. Electricity is not property that can be stolen, but is covered by the separate offence of abstracting electricity under s.13. Water flowing freely over or under ground is not property. While corpses were traditionally regarded as not capable of being property (although they may be covered by the **Human Tissue Act 1961** and the **Anatomy Act 1984**), parts of corpses may be considered to be property if their essential character and value has changed (*R* v *Kelly and Another*, 1998). Samples of blood and urine (and therefore possibly sperm) can also be included (*R* v *Rothery*, 1976).

Belonging to another

Section 5 gives detail in a number of subsections as to when property is to be regarded as belonging to another and it provides valuable assistance in determining the presence or absence of a theft.

According to s.5(1):

> Property shall be regarded as belonging to any person having possession or control of it, or having in it any proprietary right or interest (not being an equitable interest arising only from an agreement to transfer or grant an interest).

As a result, a person may be guilty of stealing from a variety of people besides simply the rightful owner of the property, for example those:

- in legitimate, actual possession of the property (*R v Turner (No. 2)*, 1971)
- in control of the goods (even where it appears that nobody actually owns the property) (*R v Woodman*, 1974)
- with any proprietary right or interest (*Waverley BC v Fletcher*, 1995)

However, by s.5(1) it also appears that it will not be theft where the person 'stolen' from has only an equitable interest arising from an agreement to transfer property — for example, where the vendor of a house agrees a sale to one party and then sells to another. It appears that it will not include a 'constructive trust' of property where the defendant has used the victim's facilities to make a secret profit (*A-G's Reference (No. 1 of 1985)*, 1986).

Section 5(2) deals with property held on trust:

> Where property is subject to a trust, the person to whom it belongs shall be regarded as including any person having a right to enforce the trust, and an intention to defeat the trust shall be regarded accordingly as an intention to deprive of the property any person having that right.

In practice, this will only apply where a trust has no recognised beneficiaries, e.g. a charitable trust. All other trust property would be recognised under s.5(1) as belonging to another.

Under s.5(3):

> Where a person receives property from or on account of another, and is under an obligation to the other to retain and deal with that property or its proceeds in a particular way, the property or proceeds shall be regarded (as against him) as belonging to the other.

Trusts, bailments and liens are normally covered by s.5(1). Therefore, s.5(3) is a fall-back provision to cover those situations where legal title to the property passes to the defendant, who is then under a strict obligation to deal with the property in a particular way. There must be an obligation to deal in a particular way (*R v Hall*, 1973), although this need not arise in a business context (*Davidge v Bunnett*, 1984). It may arise because a trust is created of the property (*R v Wain*, 1995), and s.5(3) may arise even where the purpose for which the property is to be used is fairly general (*R v Rader*, 1992).

Under s.5(4):

> Where a person gets property by another's mistake and is under an obligation to make restoration (in whole or in part) of the property or its proceeds or the value

thereof, then to the extent of that obligation the property or proceeds shall be regarded (as against him) as belonging to the person entitled to the restoration, and an intention not to make restoration shall be regarded accordingly as an intention to deprive that person of the property or proceeds.

This provision was added to reverse the effect of *Moynes* v *Cooper* (1956), so it is particularly appropriate to the overpayment of wages (*A-G's Reference (No. 1 of 1983)*, 1985 and *R* v *Stalham*, 1993). There must be a legal obligation to make restoration (*R* v *Gilks*, 1972). The provision applies equally to intangible property (*R* v *Davis*, 1988), although there has been some confusion as to whether the provision is necessary if the effect is to create a trust of the property (*R* v *Shadrokh-Cigari*, 1988).

Dishonesty

Dishonesty was chosen in the 1968 Act to describe the defendant's *mens rea* as a word that jurors would find easy to recognise and understand.

There is no actual definition of dishonesty in the Act, although there are three partial, negative definitions under s.2(1):

A person's appropriation of property belonging to another is not to be regarded as dishonest —
(a) if he appropriates the property in the belief that he has in law the right to deprive the other of it, on behalf of himself or a third person (*R* v *Small*, 1987); or
(b) if he appropriates the property in the belief that he would have the other's consent if the other knew of the appropriation and the circumstances of it (*R* v *Flynn*, 1970); or
(c) (except where the property came to him as trustee or personal representative) if he appropriates property in the belief that the person to whom the property belongs cannot be found by taking reasonable steps

This is supplemented by s.2(2): 'A person's appropriation of property may be dishonest notwithstanding that he is willing to pay for the property.' This is clearly aimed at those situations where the defendant knows that the victim has no intention of parting with his/her property but the defendant is still insistent on obtaining it.

None of this really helps in determining what dishonesty is, and who should determine it — the judge or the jury. It was established in *R* v *Feely* (1973) that, since dishonesty is a word of common usage, it is a question of fact for the jury to determine using the 'current standards of ordinary decent people' rather than for the judge to interpret.

The means of assessing dishonesty is the two-fold test in *R* v *Ghosh* (1982): 'The accused is dishonest if his conduct is dishonest according to the current standards of ordinary decent people and if the accused knows that his conduct is dishonest according to those standards.' So the test is in two parts:
- The jury must assess the defendant's behaviour according to objective standards of honesty; if the defendant is not dishonest according to those standards he should be acquitted.

- If the defendant is dishonest according to that objective standard, the jury must apply the subjective second part of the test — whether the defendant realised that it would be considered dishonest.

However, the test is generally considered unsatisfactory and has led to a number of criticisms:

- It fails to eradicate the potential for inconsistency between juries.
- There is no single standard of honesty.
- Defendants who have different social standards, in theory ought to be able to get an acquittal.
- In effect this is allowing a mistake of law to be used as a defence, which would not be the case elsewhere.
- The test is too sophisticated to ask of a jury.
- Professor Griew has argued that while dishonesty is clearly a test for the jury, this should only be with the guidance of law, and so it should be a test of law not of fact.

The intention to permanently deprive

This was the element of the offence introduced to distinguish between the criminal law and the civil law. It effectively removes illicit 'borrowing' from the scope of theft, as this can be dealt with more effectively in civil law (R v Warner, 1970).

According to s.6(1) of the **Theft Act 1968**:

> A person appropriating property belonging to another without meaning the other permanently to lose the thing itself is nevertheless to be regarded as having the intention of permanently depriving the other of it if his intention is to treat the thing as his own to dispose of regardless of the other's rights; and a borrowing or lending of it may amount to so treating it if, but only if, the borrowing or lending is for a period or in circumstances making it equivalent to an outright taking or disposal.

In the case of a 'borrowing or lending', the intention could only be proved where the goods are returned in a fundamentally changed state so that their utility is lost (R v Lloyd, 1985). A 'disposal' must mean something more than merely using someone else's property, although the dictionary definition 'to get rid of' is too restrictive (DPP v Lavender, 1994), and what makes something equivalent to an outright disposal is for the jury to decide (R v Coffey, 1987).

According to s.6(2) of the **Theft Act 1968**:

> Without prejudice to the generality of subsection (1) above, where a person, having possession or control (lawfully or not) of property belonging to another, parts with the property under a condition as to its return which he may not be able to perform, this (if done for the purposes of his own and without the other's authority) amounts to treating the property as his own to dispose of regardless of the other's rights.

This is obviously designed to cover situations such as pawning other people's property or gambling with it, or using it as security for a loan.

Robbery

Robbery is an unusual offence because it is not only a theft offence, but it also has connections with offences against the person. In essence, robbery is a theft that is achieved through the use of force, and therefore it is an aggravated form of theft. As such, it is a serious offence and it is triable only on indictment, with a maximum sentence of life imprisonment — it is treated so seriously because of its links with social alarm and protection of the public. There is also a separate crime called 'assault with intent to rob'.

Definition of robbery

The offence of robbery is found in s.8 of the **Theft Act 1968**, where according to s.8(1):

> A person is guilty of robbery if he steals, and immediately before or at the time of doing so, he uses force on any person or puts or seeks to put any person in fear of being then and there subjected to force.

The further offence of 'assault with intent to rob', the mode of trial and the maximum sentence are found in s.8(2).

Robbery is a theft offence, so all of the elements of theft must be shown to be present, as well as those elements specific to robbery (*R* v *Robinson*, 1977). However, the theft, and therefore the robbery, may be complete as soon as the defendant dispossesses the other of the property (*Corcoran* v *Anderton*, 1980).

The *actus reus* of the robbery is:
- the *actus reus* of theft (appropriation of property belonging to another)
- with force, or the threat of force
- before or at the time of the theft

The *mens rea* of robbery is:
- the *mens rea* of theft (dishonesty plus the intention to permanently deprive)
- the intentional or reckless application of force

Force

The **Theft Act** contains no specific definition of force, but the courts have accepted only minimal force to be sufficient for the offence (*R* v *Dawson*, 1976). What amounts to force is to be left to the jury to decide; force applied to property may be sufficient in certain circumstances, e.g. the wrenching away of a bag from the victim in *R* v *Clouden* (1987), although the Criminal Law Revision Committee's 8th report expressed doubts as to whether this should amount to robbery. Force directly applied to the person presents no problems (*R* v *Hale*, 1978), even when the force is carried out by one person and the theft by another. The force must be used in order to steal. If it is for some other purpose, it may be an assault or a wounding offence, but it cannot be robbery (*R* v *Donaghy*, 1981). Force also includes putting a person in fear of force. Force will usually be applied to the victim of the theft, but it need not necessarily be applied to that person, as long as it is used to steal.

Immediately before or at the time of the theft

A strict, literal interpretation of this provision would have a limiting effect on the offence, so the provision should possibly mean that the force has a direct bearing on the commission of the theft offence. Certainly force after, and unconnected with, the theft will not amount to robbery (*R* v *Gregory*, 1983), although it may do so if it is part of the struggle to escape. This depends on 'appropriation' being seen as a continuing act (*Hale*, 1978). Force used to prevent the alarm being raised may be similarly appropriate (*R* v *Lockley*, 1995).

Burglary

Burglary is an old offence with its origins in the Middle Ages. It derived from '*burge breche*', which was a form of breaking and entering at night with the intent to commit a felony. In this way, common-law principles of trespass are at the heart of the offence. The original character of the offence meant that it was always treated more seriously than mere theft because of the extra distress caused to the victim. Consequently, the offence of burglary developed very much in line with early common-law property values. The previous range of offences was limited and complex, so these were reformed in the **Theft Act 1968** and are now contained in s.9, although significantly, there are two separate offences. The offence of burglary is triable either way, for obvious reasons.

The offences of burglary

According to s.9(1):

> A person is guilty of burglary if:
> (a) he enters any building or part of a building as a trespasser and with intent to commit any such offence as is mentioned in s.9(2); or
> (b) having entered any building or part of a building as a trespasser, he steals or attempts to steal anything in the building or that part of it or inflicts or attempts to inflict on any person therein any grievous bodily harm

According to s.9(2):

> The offences referred to in subsection (1)(a) above are the offences of stealing anything in the building or part of a building in question, of inflicting on any person therein any grievous bodily harm, and of doing any unlawful damage to the building or anything therein.

Section 9 therefore creates two offences — one involving entering the premises with the intent to commit further offences identified in s.9(2), and the other where the defendant, having entered as a trespasser, goes on to commit one or more offences of a more restrictive range.

The *actus reus* in either offence involves an entry amounting to a trespass into a building or part of a building. In addition, in the case of s.9(1)(b), since one or more of the offences of theft, attempted theft, grievous bodily harm and attempted grievous bodily harm must also be committed, the *actus reus* of that offence will also have to be shown.

The *mens rea* differs between the two offences in that:
- In s.9(1)(a) the intention to commit one or more of the offences identified in s.9(2) must be shown.
- In s.9(1)(b) there is no ulterior intent, but the necessary *mens rea* is required for the offence that the defendant carries on to commit.

In either case, intention or recklessness as to the trespass must also be shown.

Burglary, like other theft offences, is very much open to interpretation and most of the terminology used has caused problems at one time or another.

The definition of building

The meaning of 'building' is not absolutely defined in the Act but it is partly expanded upon in s.9(4):

> References in subsections (1) and (2) above to a building…shall apply also to an inhabited vehicle or vessel, and shall apply to any such vehicle or vessel at times when the person having a habitation in it is not there as well as at times when he is.

It has been said that the imperfection of human language makes it not only difficult, but impossible, to define the word 'building' with any kind of accuracy. In *Stevens* v *Gourley* (1859), Byles J concluded that a building was a '…structure of considerable size and intended to be permanent or at least to endure for a considerable time'. Nevertheless, the courts continue to have difficulty in determining what the term 'building' includes. Various 'structures' have been the subject of discussion in relation to burglary. Whether or not they are 'buildings' may depend on their general character as well as on the use to which they are put — compare for instance, *Norfolk Constabulary* v *Seekings and Gould* (1986) with *B and S* v *Leathley* (1979). More problematic, of course, are temporary structures, such as caravans.

The trespass can also be to part of a building (*R* v *Walkington*, 1979), even though the building has been entered lawfully. It is important to prove, therefore, that although the defendant has entered lawfully, he/she then moved unlawfully to a part of the building, which amounts to a trespass (*R* v *Laing*, 1995).

The meaning of entry

An entry is a key requirement of the offence. In s.9(1)(a) the defendant 'enters' with intent to commit specific crimes, and in s.9(1)(b) 'having entered' the defendant goes on to commit prescribed crimes. In either case, there is no offence without an actual entry into the premises.

The obvious question is the extent to which the defendant has entered the building. In other words, does all of his/her body have to enter or only part of his/her body? Traditionally, the entry had to be 'effective and substantial' (*R v Collins*, 1972). More recently, however, the courts have been prepared to accept that there can be an 'effective' entry without the need for it to be 'substantial' (*R v Brown*, 1985). In certain circumstances it is clear that the entry need be neither 'effective' nor 'substantial' in order for the offence to be applied (*R v Ryan*, 1996). In the latter case, it was the intention of the defendant that was seen to be more important than his/her ability to carry out the ulterior offence.

The requirement of a trespass

The previous law focused on a 'breaking and entering', but the **Theft Act** replaced this with the requirement of a trespass. Trespass is really a concept associated with civil law and, although trespass is a complex area, it generally involves entering without permission, whether intentionally, recklessly or negligently. Therefore, if a person enters with permission he cannot be a trespasser (*Collins*, 1972). However, it may be considered a trespass where a person has permission to enter but acts in a way that is inconsistent with that permission (*R v Jones and Smith*, 1977).

The ulterior offences

The ulterior offences identified in s.9(2) (theft, GBH and criminal damage) can cause certain problems. It may be possible that a conditional intent to steal will be sufficient (*Attorney General's References (Nos 1 and 2 of 1979)*, 1979). Similarly, with 'inflicting grievous bodily harm', in s.9(1)(b), it is arguable that no offence need be committed (Purchas LJ in *R v Jenkins*, 1983).

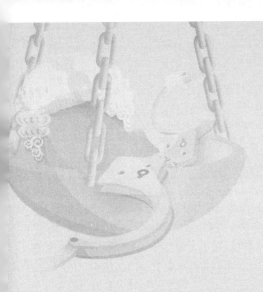

Questions
&
Answers

This section provides you with questions from Section A (essays), Section B (problems) and Section C (objective questions) on most areas of the Unit G153 specification content. Section A and B questions are marked out of 50, with 25 marks available for the knowledge that you show (AO1), 20 marks available for your ability to analyse and evaluate the law (essays) or apply the legal principles to factual situations (problems) (AO2), and 5 marks available for your communication skills (AO3). Section C questions have 20 marks available for analysis and evaluation (AO2).

A- and C-grade answers are provided for most questions. The A-grade answers should give you a clear idea of the approach and structure required. They are comprehensive in the knowledge demonstrated and show high-level evaluation or application skills. The C-grade answers tend to be quite knowledgeable but do not have the same levels of sophistication in the other skills. E-grade answers (not included) are often sketchy, with some knowledge shown but not all the necessary knowledge. They also tend to include some errors of law, and the evaluation or application skills are usually quite poor.

You should not take the A-grade responses as being model answers for you to learn off by heart; the questions in the exam will be different to those presented here. Instead, you should try to give your own answers to the questions first, and then compare them with the answers here to see what you are doing well and where you can make improvements.

Examiner's comments

Each answer is accompanied by examiner's comments, preceded by the icon *e*. These indicate where credit has been given, recognising the candidate's use of the examinable skills, as explained in the introduction. Section A questions, as well as requiring good AO1 skills of recall of knowledge, also require good essay-writing skills for AO2. Section B questions likewise require good knowledge for AO1 but concentrate on the AO2 skill of application of law. Section C questions involve pure legal reasoning and so are all AO2. Remember too the AO3 objective, which calls for effective communicative skills, use of appropriate legal terminology and correct spelling, punctuation and grammar.

In the C-grade answers the examiner points to possible improvements that could be made to achieve a higher grade. The most effective way of using this section of the book is to read the source material, read the questions, answer them, and then compare your answer with those provided to see what you are doing right and how you might improve.

Question 1

Critically consider whether the law governing involuntary manslaughter is in a satisfactory state.

■ ■ ■

A-grade answer

Involuntary manslaughter involves death where the *mens rea* of murder is not present. There are two major types of manslaughter: constructive act manslaughter (unlawful act manslaughter) and gross negligence manslaughter.

Constructive manslaughter has the same *actus reus* as for murder, i.e. you need to cause death to a human, but there are also three additional *actus reus* elements.

First, there has to be an unlawful act — this has to be an act and not an omission. This is shown in the case of *R v Lowe*. In this case there was a neglected child who died. It could not be considered constructive manslaughter as the death was caused by an omission (duty through family relationship).

Second, the act has to be specifically unlawful. *R v Lamb* concerns two friends. One of the men shot the other, although both thought that the gun would not fire. Because both defendants did not think it would fire, there was no fear of harm and therefore no assault, so this means that there could be no unlawful act.

The last element is that the act must be dangerous. The case of *R v Church* demonstrates this. The defendant attempted to have sex with a woman. When he could not satisfy her, she slapped him, and he then knocked her unconscious. Thinking she was dead, he put her in a river and she drowned. Basically, the act is dangerous if there is a risk of some harm resulting from it. This foresight must be able to be seen by a reasonable and sober person.

R v Goodfellow says that the act does not need to be aimed at a person and that it can be aimed at a property, provided that a reasonable, sober person can foresee that it would cause another person at least the risk of some harm.

The case of *R v Dawson* involved a robbery of a petrol station. When the elderly attendant pressed the alarm, the defendant fled. Following this, the attendant had a heart attack and died. The defendant's conviction was quashed because he did not know about the attendant's condition. The risk of harm had to be physical and not just fear or apprehension. This case was distinguished by *R v Watson*, where the courts said the act became dangerous as soon as the elderly man's frailty became obvious.

The *mens rea* of constructive manslaughter is the *mens rea* of the unlawful act. The defendant does not need to know the act is unlawful and dangerous.

Gross negligence manslaughter has three elements: duty of care, breach of duty causing death, and gross negligence. There are five common-law duty relationships, but the extent of the term 'duty' is unclear. Examples of duty relationships include duty through contract (*Adomako*), duty through creation of a dangerous situation (*Miller*) and duty through family relationship. Breach applies to where the defendant's conduct has gone below the standards of a normal, sober person. This can be illustrated through the case of *Stone and Dobinson*. The defendants had undertaken to look after their ill relative. The relative died and the defendants were convicted. They had breached their duty. This can be quite harsh, as in this case both defendants had exceptionally low intellect and did attempt to get help. They failed to, due to their lack of ability rather than their lack of care. Their efforts were below the standards of the reasonable person. This is exceptionally harsh and should be modified.

Gross negligence is explained through *Bateman*. In *Bateman* it was said that negligence had to have gone beyond a matter of compensation, showing a distinct lack of regard for life and deserving punishment. This test has been approved in *Adomako* but it is not known how the jury will interpret it.

The current law on involuntary manslaughter has been heavily criticised. The courts' confusion over liability in terms of a negligence-based system of fault or a recklessness-based system of fault has caused instability and a lack of clarity in the law. Due to the case of *Lidar*, there are now three aspects of liability concerning involuntary manslaughter, but given the history of the courts in this area, how long it will last is unknown.

The courts have had problems with defining what constitutes an unlawful act. Cases like *Dias*, *Kennedy*, *Dalby* and *Bland* all show inconsistency and a lack of clarity. There has also been a gap in the existing law and defendants may escape liability. This is demonstrated in *Khan and Khan*. Drug dealers escaped liability because no unlawful act had occurred and there was no duty.

One set of reforms has been suggested by Glanville Williams, who said that gross negligence manslaughter should be abolished, as negligence is not sufficient for a crime as serious as manslaughter.

This area has been looked at a number of times by law reform bodies. In particular, the Law Commission has drafted dramatic changes in this area, calling for a replacement of gross negligence and unlawful act manslaughter. They are to be changed to reckless killing and killing by gross carelessness. These changes represent the current unsatisfactory state of involuntary manslaughter, as they are a dramatic shift from the current law. However, these reforms have not been implemented, so the current unsatisfactory law remains.

e This is a comprehensive answer. The candidate introduces the essay in a succinct manner. There is a strong focus on relevant case law, with the cases being used in an appropriate manner. The candidate supports his/her points well, rather than providing an exhaustive list detailing the case acts. The candidate focuses predominantly on knowledge (AO1) throughout the essay and does not focus on AO2 until the later part of the essay. Although this is satisfactory, some candidates may forget towards the end of the essay to include all the relevant evaluative comments. The only significant criticism of this candidate's work is the limited discussion of the Law Commission's changes. However, the conclusion is commendable for using the question as its focus.

∎∎∎

C-grade answer

Involuntary manslaughter involves death but the *mens rea* of murder is not present as there is no intent. There are different types of involuntary manslaughter: constructive act manslaughter (also known as unlawful act manslaughter) and gross negligence manslaughter. There is also the element of reckless manslaughter, because without reckless manslaughter there is a gap of liability. This is seen with *Khan* v *Khan*.

In constructive act manslaughter, there are both *mens rea* and *actus reus* elements. The *mens rea* element is the *mens rea* of an unlawful act. The defendant does not have to know that the act is unlawful and dangerous, as per *Newbury* v *Jones*.

The *actus reus* elements of constructive act manslaughter are the unlawful act and the fact that the act must be dangerous. The unlawful act has to be an act and not an omission, as per *Lowe*, and it also needs to be unlawful, as per *Lamb*, where it was held that there must be fear of an assault. This is therefore justifying the defendant's actions, which is not satisfactory for the crime, so the law needs to be reformed in this area.

There is then the need for the act to be dangerous, which is an objective test. As in *Church*, the defendant must foresee a risk of harm. It was held that an act must be dangerous if there were an objective risk of some harm, and the risk must be foreseeable by a reasonable and sober person. This was modified by *Dawson*, which allowed the victim's characteristics to be accounted for.

There have been some problems with this. *R* v *Goodfellows* shows that the act need not be aimed at a person — this is surely justifying the death of someone through a threat that does not directly endanger one's life.

For constructive act manslaughter, the defendant must apply to the rules of causation: he must be the factual cause and the legal cause with no intervening act. The death must also be of a human being.

Gross negligence manslaughter has three elements to it. These are breach of duty of care, breach of duty causing death and gross negligence.

Duty of care is the relationship from omissions. This is signified with *R* v *Adomako*: when someone fails to perform a contract and it endangers life. It can also be seen with *Stone and Dobinson*. The exact terms of duty are unclear and this part of the law needs reform.

Breach of duty causing death means that the defendant's act has gone below the standard expected of the reasonable, sober person.

For gross negligence it must have gone beyond a matter of compensation, showing a distinct lack of regard for life (as in *Bateman*). This area is in a satisfactory state for the governing law body.

The scope of the duty relationship has been criticised, as its application is too narrow.

The area of involuntary manslaughter is in need of reform. One area to be reformed would be to introduce corporate manslaughter to make companies more responsible, as they are currently not taking full responsibility.

Another proposed change is to involve the offences of reckless killing and also killing by gross carelessness. This was proposed in 1994 by the Law Reforms Commission.

> The candidate introduces the area by discussing the difference between murder and involuntary manslaughter. He/she then discusses the current law concerning gross negligence manslaughter and unlawful act manslaughter, outlining the major principles in this area with appropriate case citation. In parts, the candidate makes sporadic comments regarding the effectiveness of certain aspects of the current law. The candidate makes an attempt at the end to focus on AO2 issues, but these are limited and lack development. There is also no conclusion. What the candidate has done is to discuss what he/she knows about the law regarding involuntary manslaughter but has failed to address the set question. He/she has also failed to take into account the blend of AO1 and AO2 and, as a consequence, this would limit considerably the marks available.

Question 2

'It seems unreasonable to expect the ordinary person to behave like a hero when confronted with a threat of death or serious harm unless he/she agrees to commit or join in a crime. On the other hand, public policy demands that some form of resistance to such a threat must be encouraged by our law.'

Consider whether the courts have successfully developed the defence of duress by threats in order to balance these apparently conflicting concerns.

■ ■ ■

A-grade answer

Duress is a common-law defence. It is a complete defence to all crimes, with the exception of murder and attempted murder. The defence of duress has caused the judiciary a number of problems and it continues to do so as the courts struggle to get the balance of the defence correct.

Duress is a defence based on a concession to human frailty. It allows a defendant to claim that the reason why he/she committed a crime was that he/she was forced to carry it out due to threats of death or serious injury from another party.

Duress by threats can only be used if certain conditions are satisfied. First, there needs to be a threat. This threat, according to *Whelan*, must be an immediate threat of death or serious injury.

At whom must the threat be directed? This has been steadily widened by the courts. According to *Wright*, the threat can be aimed at the defendant, his/her family or friends. This therefore allows a wide range of people to be threatened and the accused can use the defence of duress. The courts' position on this is similar to the Law Commission's view, in that they believe that there should be no restrictions on the person being threatened.

The threat also needs some immediacy. This is due to the fact that the defendant could escape or seek police protection. The courts have taken a liberal view on the timescale regarding immediacy. In *Hudson and Taylor*, the defendant's conviction was quashed on appeal because the issue regarding protection was not left to the jury. In *Abdul-Hussain*, the courts stated that the threat only had to be imminent and not immediate. This is again a change by the courts that has benefited the defendant.

The threat must also be of death or serious injury. This was confirmed in *Valderrama-Vega*, where the defendant was threatened by drug gangs that his family would be hurt unless he smuggled drugs. There were also two other threats, one connected with money and the other with a revelation regarding the defendant's homosexuality. The courts reinforced the fact that the threat had to be of death or serious injury, but it also stated that it did not have to be the sole reason for acting.

question

There therefore have to be severe threats to allow the defence of duress. This can be harsh on certain defendants. What about threats to property or threats directed towards pets? The courts have refused to extend this area but there are moral and legal arguments that this aspect of the defence should be modified.

The defendant also needs to satisfy the Graham test. This includes a subjective and objective test — the defendant must believe the threat of death and a reasonable person with the defendant's characteristics would have acted the same.

In looking at the objective test, there are certain characteristics that can be taken into account. According to *Bowen*, the following characteristics are relevant: age, pregnancy, serious physical disability, recognised mental illness or psychiatric condition and sex. *Bowen* excluded self-induced characteristics, e.g. alcohol, drugs or glue sniffing.

The issue of characteristics has been called into question. It is argued that there should be a wider range of characteristics allowed. The courts are harsher in this area than they are for provocation. *Morhall* gives more flexibility to the defendant in terms of acceptable characteristics.

The defence of duress is not allowed if the defendant has voluntarily joined a gang. This includes associating with people of a criminal nature. This only applies, according to *R v Z*, if the defendant can foresee that particular type of threat. The courts have had considerable problems in this area. The courts have shown a lack of sympathy to those who get themselves involved in crime, especially drug-related crime. The courts have also been unsure about where to draw the line regarding the law. The law has changed numerous times and is likely to change again.

Duress of threats is also not available for murder, attempted murder or being an accessory to murder. This was decided in the cases of *Howe* and *Gotts*. Lord Hailsham in particular was strongly opposed to duress being available in this area. He thought it would give a defence to cowards, and believed that a defendant should take his/her own life instead. This is a very unrealistic approach. Would an individual really take his/her own life when faced with the death of a stranger? Hailsham also failed to consider situations where taking one life could save the lives of many.

Lord Hailsham's views are not supported by the Law Commission. It believes that duress should be available for all crimes, including murder.

The courts have had a number of difficulties regarding duress of threats. It has been difficult for them to get the balance right with the defence. There have been calls by some judges for Parliament to intervene and put the defence on a statutory footing. This would help in determining the scope of the defence and dictate how much resistance is needed to stand up to a threat. Without this intervention the courts will continue to struggle to find the right balance with the defence.

This is a thorough and detailed response, showing a breadth of knowledge regarding duress of threats. Some aspects of the defence are thinly discussed but the candidate has dealt with a wide range of issues and cases. It may have been appropriate to use case facts in certain areas, as this can help in the explanation required for AO2. For example, the case facts of *Hudson and Taylor* illustrate why the courts had sympathy for the defendants.

High AO2 marks would be awarded for a number of reasons. The candidate discusses the merits of particular legal principles, suggests reforms and highlights law reform proposals. The candidate would also achieve high AO3 marks for the quality of his/her written communication.

■ ■ ■

C-grade answer

The defence of duress is available to most people who are forced into committing a crime. However, there are strict guidelines regarding the nature of the threat. There are two defences of duress: one of threats and one of circumstances. This question deals with duress of threats. The difference between duress of threats and duress of circumstances is that the threat has to be nominated. This is dealt with in the case of *Cole*.

For the defence of duress to be available, the threat in the case must be that of death or serious injury. As seen in the case of *Valderrama-Vega*, the threat to expose sexual orientation does not count.

The threat also has to be towards the defendant or his/her family, or a person for whom he/she feels responsible in his/her current situation (*Ortiz*).

The final thing that gives the person the defence of duress is if he/she satisfies the principle in the Graham test: the jury must be sure that the defendant feared death or serious injury (subjective test), and it also has to be decided whether the reasonable person sharing the same characteristics of the defendant (age, gender etc.) would have feared death or serious injury in the same situation.

If the defendant satisfies these criteria, he/she is given the defence of duress. However, there are three things that can take away the defence. The first is the test of imminence. If the threat is not immediate or close to immediate, the defendant will not be allowed the defence, e.g. *Hussain and Others* where the defence was rejected because the defendants' aggressors were in a different country.

The second thing is escape. If the defendant does not attempt to take an escape opportunity when it is presented, he/she will be denied a defence.

The last thing that can take away a defence of duress is voluntary exposure. If a person voluntarily exposes him/herself to a situation where he/she could be forced to commit a crime, he/she will be denied a defence of duress.

Another issue with duress is that it is not a defence to murder. It is expected that if a person is forced to kill someone he/she will be a hero and take his/her own life instead. Asking a person to take his/her own life seems unreasonable because it is expected that most people will take the life of another in order to save their own lives.

The candidate demonstrates a solid appreciation of the legal principles regarding duress. He/she uses a number of cases to support arguments and illustrate points. However, compared to the A-grade answer, fewer issues are discussed and the level of detail is not as comprehensive.

There are sufficient AO1 comments to use as a springboard to develop AO2, but AO2 comments are sparse and the candidate should have developed this area. It is important to have a balance: AO2 carries 20 marks out of the possible 50.

Question 3

'English law does not, in general, impose liability for a failure to act, despite the fact that there may be compelling moral justifications for doing so. For example, the courts have often explained that there is no legal duty upon a stranger to rescue a drowning child.'

Assess the truth of this statement and consider whether the current principles governing liability for omissions are satisfactory.

■ ■ ■

A-grade answer

An omission is a failure to act — for example, you watch a person drown. In criminal law there is no criminal liability for failure to act, although there are two exceptions. First, there are statutory exceptions, which are normally strict liability offences. An example of this would be refusing to take a breath test, when asked to do so by the police. Second, there are common-law exceptions, and this occurs when the court decides you are under a duty to act.

An omission is part of the *actus reus* for certain crimes, e.g. murder and gross negligence manslaughter. Certain crimes cannot be done via an omission, e.g. unlawful act manslaughter and robbery.

As the question states, English law imposes no general duty on people to help each other out or to save anyone from harm. Therefore, you can watch a drowning child in certain circumstances and have no legal liability. However, the courts will uphold legal liability for a failure to act if there was a duty. There are currently five situations that are duty situations.

Duty through contract is when a person has a positive duty to act due to a contract. It normally arises when a failure to perform your contract endangers life. Therefore, lifeguards and doctors can be held criminally liable for failure to perform their contracts. This was shown in the case of *R* v *Pittwood*, where a gatekeeper of a railway line went for lunch, leaving the gate open. A hay cart crossed the line and was hit by a train. One man was killed and another was seriously injured. The defendant was convicted of manslaughter based on a failure to carry out his contract to close the gate when a train was approaching.

Cases like *Pitwood* and *Adomako* have liability imposed because you are paid to perform a set task and if you fail to perform it you should be responsible. However, academics like Ashworth question the need for criminal liability in these circumstances and think the civil law and compensation are more appropriate than criminal sanctions.

Duty through public office is shown in the case of *R* v *Dytham*, where a uniformed policeman saw a man being kicked to death. The policeman took no steps to intervene and drove away quickly when the violence was over. The defendant was convicted of wilfully, and without reasonable excuse, neglecting to perform a duty to protect the victim. Criminal liability is imposed here because the courts consider that those in positions of public trust should achieve certain standards of behaviour.

Duty from family relationships is shown in *Gibbons and Proctor*. Gibbons was cohabiting with Proctor and all their children. However, one child, of whom Proctor was not the natural mother, was kept separate from the rest and ill-treated by Gibbons. The child starved to death. Gibbons owed the child a duty through family relationship and was convicted. This area is considered so important that it has been placed on a statutory footing.

Assumption of a duty of care is shown above as Proctor was convicted of manslaughter. The idea of duty of care is shown in depth by *Stone and Dobinson*. The husband and wife were of low intelligence. They took Stone's sister into their home, providing her with a bed. However, she became ill. She wasn't fed and she developed bed sores and eventually died as a result of this. The two defendants tried to ring a doctor but were of low intelligence and didn't know how to use a telephone. They were convicted of manslaughter, as the defendants had been under a common-law duty and failed to carry it out.

The case of *Stone and Dobinson* shows how harsh the duties can be on the defendant. People are liable who should not be. The defendants did try to help Stone's sister and did their best considering their low level of intellect. This case does not demonstrate a need for criminal liability via omissions — it is morally unjust that they were convicted and sent to prison.

A duty can also arise when you create a dangerous situation. This is shown in the case of *R v Miller*. If you start a situation which results in harm, you are liable if you become aware of the situation and fail to take steps to minimise the harm.

The duty scenarios have been heavily criticised by some people. There appears to be an inconsistency. How can a person of low intelligence be liable, but not a person who watches a child drown? All it would take to discharge would be a phone call.

This area is treated differently in other legal systems. For example, France has a 'Good Samaritan' law, which means that strangers owe a duty of care. The Good Samaritan law makes it an offence not to act in certain circumstances.

This area is inconsistent, as there is no reason why some relationships have arisen and others have not. In addition, why do some occupations have a duty and some do not? The courts have sometimes called a situation that is an omission an act (*Fagan*), and an act an omission (*Bland*). This has not helped this area of the law.

There is a reluctance to form new duty relationships, for example *Khan and Khan* where drug dealers watched as one of their clients died. They were not liable to act as they had no duty to act.

To conclude, there are problems with the law on omissions. This has not been helped by the judiciary, who have developed the law on a case-by-case basis without any logical order or plan. There is a need to review this area systematically but on legal lines, not moral ones. The law can only be shaped on moral lines by Parliament, whose members are elected by the people, and it is not for the judiciary to dictate moral boundaries.

🖉 This is a very strong response given the time constraints and the pressurised conditions. There is a clear explanation of the legal concepts and principles surrounding this area. The concepts are supported by appropriate case law, with the candidate using a variety of cases and discussing them at an appropriate level.

The candidate makes a range of AO2 points. There is a discussion of the legal principles, not only in terms of the merits and defects of the duty but also regarding the topic as a whole.

The essay has a clear introduction, main body and conclusion. AO3 criteria are well met in this response. The candidate refers and responds to the question throughout, and concludes with the quote in mind.

Question 4

Evaluate the effectiveness of intoxication as a defence.

■ ■ ■

A-grade answer

Intoxication is a complicated defence. It can result in a complete acquittal in certain circumstances, but in others it cannot diminish liability. The reason for the inconsistent approach is that the defence has been shaped by public policy. The rules of intoxication are dictated by whether the defendant was voluntarily or involuntarily intoxicated and if the crime committed was a basic or specific intent crime.

For the defence of intoxication, the defendant must bring evidence of the intoxication. This is effective in allowing the defence only a narrow application because it has to be proved, although there is a distinction that can be seen between drugs and alcohol.

For the defence of intoxication, the defendant has to show that he/she was so intoxicated as to be unable to form the *mens rea* due to the effect of drink or drugs. There is a difference between voluntary and involuntary intoxication, however. In the case of *Kingston*, the defendant was involuntarily intoxicated. However, a narrow application of the defence was used and so although Kingston did not intoxicate himself, he still received the same sentence as somebody who was voluntarily intoxicated and who had committed the same offence. This is because he was able to form the *mens rea*. An intoxicated intent is still intent. This is a harsh decision, as the defendant was set up and was involuntarily intoxicated. It may be due to the type of crime the defendant was involved in, and it was a public policy decision.

The defence of intoxication will only work in specific circumstances if the defendant is voluntarily intoxicated. The defence will work regarding specific intent crimes but not regarding basic intent crimes. A specific intent crime is one that has intent alone as the *mens rea* requirement. Examples include murder and GBH with intent. Although this appears to be a good defence, the defendant will be charged with a lesser crime as in *Lipman*.

In relation to basic intent crimes, voluntary intoxication cannot be used as a defence. This was confirmed in the case of *DPP* v *Majewski*. Basic intent crimes include crimes like s.20 GBH, ABH and rape.

The consequence of this is that most specific intent crimes have a directly related lesser crime, e.g. murder to manslaughter. The prosecution will charge an individual who committed a specific intent crime when drunk with a lesser basic intent crime. Therefore, the defence will not result in the defendant having no liability. This is known as the fallback theory. There are gaps in this, for example theft. In theft there is no fallback, meaning a defendant has a complete defence. This is a loophole that should be closed.

If the defendant is intoxicated as a result of 'Dutch courage' and commits a crime, then the defence of intoxication is not allowed due to the fact that the defendant already had the *mens rea* of the crime before he/she started to become intoxicated, and the intoxication was intended to aid him/her. This was decided in the case of *Gallagher*.

Involuntary intoxication means that drinks have been spiked. This can be a defence to both basic and specific intent crimes. The courts have been liberal with the concept of involuntary intoxication. If a drug has a soporific effect, a defendant will be treated as being involuntary intoxicated. In *R v Hardie*, the defendant took Valium and committed arson. He was treated as being involuntarily intoxicated, as the drug was suppose to calm him down but did the opposite.

Intoxication is not a true defence. It works by putting doubt into the jury's mind that the defendant would not have acted as he/she did had he/she not been intoxicated. This brings the burden on the jury rather than on the defence, where it should be.

Intoxication is an effective defence as it can also be used with other defences such as insanity — defined in the M'Naghten rules — and automatism.

This defence is controversial because of the huge number of crimes committed by people who are under the influence of drink or drugs. Due to this, it has been argued that it should be abolished completely on the grounds of public policy and to act as a deterrent.

The Butler Committee adopted a different approach to intoxication. It recommended the creation of a new offence of dangerous intoxication. It would only carry 1 year's punishment. It had few supporters. Given the range of crimes it would cover, it would be an easy way out. One year for murder?

There has also been criticism of the basic intent and specific intent divide. This is due to the fact that what is basic and what is specific is not easily decided.

This defence is significant in the UK due to the vast number of people who become intoxicated and then become involved in crime. It has been developed with public policy in mind. However, it is now time to seriously review it.

🖉 This essay shows a strong understanding of the major themes regarding intoxication and includes a variety of cases and concepts. The only issue not fully explored is the effect of intoxication on other defences such as mistake and diminished responsibility. This is a major gap in the AO1.

The AO2 is well developed. There is a discussion not only on the merits of the principles but also on suggestions regarding reforms. However, this could have been developed more by considering the approach of other countries.

■ ■ ■

C-grade answer

Plan

Neg	Good
• Fallback theory	• Dutch courage
• Partial/complete defence	• Soporific *Hardie* (Valium)
• Voluntary intoxication	• Involuntary narrow
• Specific not basic	• Doesn't count 4 going on 'trips'
– *Kingston* — paedophile/homosexual. 15 yr old	
– *Baily* 19 inch cut iron bar	
– *Lipman* — LSD snakes	

As a defence, intoxication is probably one of the most flexible as it can be both a partial and a complete defence, but there are many negative outcomes that this could potentially allow.

Fallback theory, whereby if a defence of intoxication is successful the charge will be reduced to a lesser crime, can have severe implications for cases of murder, with a possible sentence difference of 15 years. Intoxication will work as a complete defence for those crimes with no fallback, such as theft and burglary, in which case the defendant will be acquitted.

In addition, the fact that voluntary intoxication is a defence for specific intent and not basic intent seems a little strange, as it means that the more violent or perverse crimes are getting a better defence than the rest.

However, the defence is made more effective in the way that 'Dutch courage' is not permitted because this would imply the *mens rea* was formed before the defendant became intoxicated.

The soporific effect, which is where drugs or alcohol are said to have a sleepy effect on people, is still quite strict, as seen in the case of *Hardie*, where after the defendant broke up with his girlfriend he took some Valium, went back to the flat and set fire to the wardrobe. He was convicted of arson and the jury was not permitted to consider the depression of the defendant or the soporific effects of the drugs.

For voluntary intoxication, the courts do not permit the excuse of being on 'a trip' for committing a crime, which is good considering the potential damage a trip could cause. This was seen in the case of *Lipman* where a couple took some LSD. The boyfriend/defendant thought that snakes were attacking the centre of the earth. When the boyfriend woke up in the morning, his girlfriend had been strangled and had inches of sheet stuffed in her mouth. The defendant was convicted for her death after much difference of opinion between the Court of Appeal and the House of Lords.

Involuntary intoxication is a narrow defence, allowing only for spiking of people's drinks and food. Although this is mostly a good thing, problems could arise when people mix medication with drink or drugs and are not aware of the effects and consequently commit a criminal offence. It is then quite hard to gather a defence as it depends on whether the defendant was sufficiently aware of the dangers of mixing the medication. However, involuntary intoxication does apply to basic and specific intent crimes.

🖉 Creating a plan before beginning to write is a sensible approach, as it allows candidates to gauge how successful they would be at answering a question and acts as a guide while writing the answer. However, an examiner would find this plan hard to follow.

The candidate explains most of the major principles but does not consistently support them with case citation. This is odd, as some of these cases are mentioned in the plan, e.g. *Kingston* and *Bailey*. Although credit would be given for the plan, it is important to refer back to a plan and to check against it when reviewing an essay.

AO2 is attempted, but the comments are sporadic and do not have the breadth or depth needed. For example, a discussion on the Law Commission's proposals or the alternatives suggested to the current law would have been appropriate.

Question 5

Stuart, a reformed heroin addict who has not taken any heroin for 2 months, is sitting in a café having a quiet drink. Hannah, an acquaintance from his drug-taking past, sees Stuart and comes over to where he is reading a newspaper. Hannah knocks the paper out of his hand and says: 'Fancy meeting you here, you old junkie.'

Stuart, who is well known for having a short temper, merely responds by picking up the paper from the floor and replying: 'What do you want?' 'I want to score some heroin from you,' Hannah responds. Stuart replies that he has kicked the habit months ago. Hannah says: 'You lying rat, you'll never be able to quit the habit; everyone knows you're a waster and a slave to drugs.' Stuart, who is in fact still suffering from heroin withdrawal symptoms, which sometimes affect his behaviour, says: 'It's true I've packed it up, now shove off!' Disgusted by this, Hannah throws the remainder of her drink in Stuart's face. Enraged, Stuart takes out a knife and stabs Hannah, killing her instantly. Stuart has now been charged with murder.

Discuss Stuart's potential liability, taking into account any defences that may be available to him.

■ ■ ■

A-grade answer

This scenario involves murder, and the defence of provocation and possibly DR, which could reduce the conviction from murder to manslaughter.

To be guilty of murder, the defendant must have caused the death of another human being, in a country of the realm, under the Queen's peace. There must also be malice aforethought, the *mens rea* element of murder, which is intention to cause death or GBH.

In this scenario, Stuart has obviously fulfilled the *actus reus* of murder and it is very likely that the jury will find the relevant *mens rea*. Even if Stuart argues he did not intend to kill, the *mens rea* of murder includes intent to cause GBH. Taking a knife and stabbing someone is clearly intent to cause GBH as a minimum. If he were convicted of murder, Stuart would receive a life sentence. However, if he successfully used the defence of provocation or diminished responsibility (DR), he would reduce the conviction to manslaughter and could potentially receive a lesser sentence.

Provocation is covered by s.3 of the Homicide Act. To use this there must be things done or said (as per *Doughty and Pearson*). Hannah has obviously done something (she threw a drink in his face) and said something, as she has made a number of abusive comments.

The defendant must have also lost his self-control. The test for this is outlined in *Duffy*, which states the loss of self-control must be sudden and temporary. There are a number of incidents in a short space of time. According to *Humphreys*, it does not have to be the last act. Given that Stuart stabs Hannah in an enraged state, it is highly likely that he will satisfy this element, but it is an issue for the jury.

The stumbling block may be the 'reasonable man test', where the jury has to decide if the reasonable man with the defendant's characteristics would have lost his self-control. The lead case for this is *Smith*, which allows the jury to take into account characteristics of the defendant. However, these characteristics are limited in the case of *Camplin*. Excluded characteristics are exceptional excitabilities, ill temper or drunkenness. In terms of Stuart, his age and sex and the withdrawal from the heroin could be taken into account, but his short temper would be excluded. It is then up to the jury to decide if the reasonable man with the defendant's allowed characteristics would have lost his self-control. If this is accepted, the defendant would be able to use the defence of provocation.

For the defence of provocation to be used in the first place, the judge must decide if there is sufficient evidence for the defence to use. This is very likely in this case. If the judge allows provocation to be argued, then it is up to the prosecution to prove beyond all reasonable doubt that there is no provocation. This means that, if there is any doubt in the jury's mind, provocation must be allowed.

To use diminished responsibility, there must be an abnormality of the mind. This is a state of mind so different from that of a normal human being that the reasonable person would term it abnormal, as decided in the case of *Byrne*. In this case, it is up to the jury to decide whether Stuart may have a defect of the mind caused by the heroin withdrawal.

The abnormality of the mind must have come from a specified cause. There are four specified causes, but none really cover withdrawal or addiction. His drug addiction may have caused depression, or the drug addiction could have caused some physical harm to the brain. Stuart therefore may be able to satisfy this element of DR.

The abnormality of the mind must substantially impair the defendant's judgement. In the case of *Lloyd*, it was stated that substantial does not mean total, but it also does not mean trivial. Again, it is up to the jury to find, but as it is very wide then it is quite easy to pass.

It is up to the judge whether to allow DR to be put to the jury, but the burden of proof rests with Stuart. It is also important that Stuart can bring medical evidence of any condition — without it, his claim for DR will most likely be rejected.

Stuart is highly likely to satisfy the *actus reus* and *mens rea* of murder. He can raise the defence of both provocation and diminished responsibility and it does not matter that he tries to use both. There are merits to both issues and it is likely that he may be successful. The crucial issue for both is the belief of the jury.

The candidate starts with a brief but appropriate introduction, outlining the major issues. This is a good way to start a problem question.

The response goes on to identify any potential liability regarding Stuart. Again, this is a good style to adopt. The answer then quickly, but correctly, identifies the major elements of murder. It does not spend too much time on elements that are clearly identified. The candidate uses appropriate elements from the question to support his/her conclusions, e.g. the discussion surrounding malice aforethought.

An insightful analysis of the defences of provocation and diminished responsibility is given. Case law is used but it is not discussed in detail. This is a correct approach, although sometimes it is appropriate to explain more regarding a case when it has similarities with the scenario. The candidate then makes informed judgements about the law in relation to the question. In certain parts, he/she gives a neutral response, such as 'it will be an issue for the jury'. This can be a valid approach if there is uncertainty as to the liability of a defendant to an aspect of the law.

There is a good blend of law and its application throughout. The response is based firmly on the question, and the use of the question to aid the answer is commendable. There is a logical order and elements are discussed in turn. AO3 is very strong.

Question 6

John is the captain of the Bluebell United football team. During a match against the team's local rivals, he is involved in an accidental clash of heads while jumping for the ball with an opposing player, Kevin. John receives a large bruise above his left eye and Kevin sustains a small graze on his eyebrow.

John insists on continuing after treatment with a cold sponge, but is obviously in a dazed condition. A few minutes later, he jumps wildly into a late challenge on Kevin. Kevin is stretchered off and X-rays later reveal he has a broken ankle. The referee, Gemma, raises a red card to send John off the pitch. In his confused state John thinks the referee is about to attack him and punches Gemma on the nose causing it to bleed.

Advise John as to his potential criminal liability.

■ ■ ■

A-grade answer

This case deals with non-fatal offences against the person, more specifically GBH; it also deals with automatism, battery and non-fatal offences in sport.

The first offence that needs to be looked at in this case is the accidental clash of heads. This involves two injuries. These are of a lower level and will concern battery, s.39 assault and battery, and ABH.

Battery as per s.39 of the Criminal Justice Act involves the application of unlawful force on another person, either intentionally or recklessly. The level of force can be minor and can involve the least touching, as long as it is hostile. This was confirmed in the case of *R v Brown*. The *mens rea* of battery is that the defendant applied force either intentionally or recklessly, and this was established in the case of *R v Venna*.

ABH is defined by s.47 of the Offences Against the Person Act. It states that there needs to be an assault that occasions actual bodily harm. This means that first there has to be an assault or battery. The level of harm has to be more than trivial and the *mens rea* is that of assault or battery.

If you consider the bruise, it can be either battery or ABH. Minor bruising is normally charged by the Crown Prosecution Service under s.39 and more extensive bruising under s.47. The question states that John received a large bruise and this makes it more likely that Kevin will be charged under s.47. Clearly, he satisfies the elements under s.47 but may be able to use the defence of consent.

A small graze is a minor injury. For s.47 the injury has to be more than trivial. This injury will therefore be a s.39 offence. However, the defence of consent needs to be considered. The defence of consent is available to people involved in contact sports. *AG Ref No 1* states this. In *Billinghurst* it states that contact is allowed, as long as it is inside the rules of the game. Clearly, jumping for the ball is inside the rules of the game and therefore consent will be available. The injuries caused to both John and Kevin will now have no liability.

The second offence that is discussed in this case is the challenge by John on Kevin. A broken ankle is a serious injury. It could be argued that this offence is outside the rules of the game and so, as a result, could be a criminal offence. This is supported by the fact that John jumps wildly into the tackle. The crime committed could either be ABH or GBH.

There are two types of GBH, s.18 and s.20, and there are two ways of achieving each offence, either by wounding or by inflicting GBH. I am not discussing wounding, as it has not happened. The *actus reus* of inflicting GBH through s.18 or s.20 is the same. The defendant has to cause GBH. GBH in *R* v *Saunders* was described as serious harm.

The *mens rea* does differ. Section 18 GBH requires intent alone and s.20 requires the infliction of some harm, either intentionally or recklessly.

The level of harm is clearly serious and was caused by John. It will depend on the *mens rea* whether it will be s.20 or s.18. This is difficult because all it states is that he went wildly into the challenge. If he did intend to cause harm, it will be a s.18 offence and could result in a maximum sentence of life, and if not it will be a s.20 offence and result in 5 years' maximum imprisonment. The situation is also made complex because of the rules on consent. Although he went wildly into a late challenge, it is not an off-the-ball incident like *Billinghurst* and, as the debate regarding Roy Keane demonstrates, this is a complex area and it would be difficult to secure a conviction.

The third offence that is committed in this case is John striking the referee, Gemma. This is another non-fatal offence against the person. When he punched her in the face he committed either ABH or GBH against her.

ABH has already been explained. There is clearly an assault that causes harm that is more than merely trivial and he does intend to hit the referee. There is therefore enough to satisfy the conditions of ABH. A cut nose could be a GBH offence, depending on how serious the injury was. A break in the continuity of the skin can amount to a wounding. There would need to be a break in the skin, as stated in *Eisenhower*. It does not state whether the nose is cut or is just bleeding, or the full extent of the injury. Therefore, there could be liability for ABH or GBH.

The main defence that can be involved in this case is automatism (*see end of essay). This is a defence that could be applied as a result of the clash of heads between John and Kevin, if it can be proved that the defendant has a total loss of self-control and a total loss of voluntary control. This is discussed in the case *Broome* v *Perkins*. The loss of control must be caused by external factors rather than the defendant's brain. This is the case here because the factor that could have caused his automatism is a clash of heads (*R* v *T*, 1990).

There is a problem with John proving that he has automatism because there is an evidential burden in establishing the defence. He must have sufficient evidence to prove to the jury that he was in an autonomic state when he challenged Kevin and also when he struck Gemma. Medical evidence will need to be brought to prove that he was in an autonomic state. If the defence is successful, it will operate as a complete defence to all of his crimes and the court will have to decide whether he is insane.

John could also argue that his dazed state caused him to become ignorant of the law and so, as such, he should have the defence of mistake. However, ignorance of the law is not a defence.

Another defence that John could use is self-defence; he could argue that when he saw Gemma raising the card he faced an imminent threat and so he reacted with reasonable force. In mistake of self-defence, the defendant is judged on the facts as he honestly believed them to be. He feared for his own safety and reacted, e.g. *Beckford v R* (1988). There is an argument that John should have reacted when he feared the assault and if he didn't he would be denied a defence. Self-defence is contained within s.3 of the Criminal Law Act, and it is up to the jury to decide whether he has a defence.

In conclusion, all of the offences and all of the defences require input from the jury to prove them. John could have committed ABH. However, he could also have defences of automatism or self-defence.

* this defence could apply to the broken ankle.

🖉 The candidate provides a wide-ranging discussion of the key issues of non-fatal offences, consent, mistaken self-defence and automatism. He/she deals with each of these issues and analyses them to varying degrees. There is mostly good use of case law to illustrate legal principles. It may have been useful for the candidate to illustrate some case facts to highlight similarities or differences between the scenario and the actual law, e.g. the use of the case facts in *Billinghurst*.

The candidate has a focused approach. He/she clearly identifies appropriate offences instead of just discussing all potential offences, and uses the scenario facts to support conclusions for AO2, which is good technique.

The response would have benefited from some planning. The introduction is clumsy and the whole answer is rather disjointed. It is also rushed in parts. Mistakes have been made with reference to the case law ('AG Ref No 1' should be 'AG Ref No 6'). However, there is evidence of some proofreading due to the addition made on automatism. Proofreading is important for two reasons — to check for spelling and grammar and to allow for reflection, which may lead to additions.

■ ■ ■

question

C-grade answer

a) John is involved in an accidental clash of heads while jumping for the ball, with an opposing player Kevin.

Key issue: consent
Due to the fact that the injury took place during a match, there is sufficient consent by both players. Both players must understand that sport may lead to injuries (*Billinghurst*).

b) John receives a large bruise above his left eye and Kevin sustains a small graze on his eyebrow.

Key issue: non-fatal offences
Kevin commits ABH. The *actus reus* is any act that causes the victim to apprehend an immediate infliction of violence or the actual infliction of violence — Kevin caused a bruise.

Occasioning: the accident caused the bruise.

Bodily harm: John got a bruise.

Mens rea: liability is established if the defendant has the *mens rea* of common assault (*Venna*) (intentional or reckless).

With a reckless challenge, no *mens rea* is required to cause ABH; all that needs to be proved is a causal link between the defendant's act and the harm.

Kevin commits battery. The *actus reus* is the infliction of unlawful force by one person to another. The accident will amount to unlawful force.

The *mens rea*: the defendant intentionally/recklessly applies force to another person.

Kevin's broken ankle is GBH — but it could be under either s.18 or s.20 of the Offences Against the Person Act. This is because John's intention is unclear, due to the fact he was in a dazed condition. He has the *actus reus* (GBH) for both offences but for s.20 his *mens rea* could be intentional or subjectively reckless, and for s.18 the *mens rea* is that he must have specific intent, i.e. to do the same GBH or to recklessly prevent a lawful arrest/detention.

Therefore, the offence depends on John's *mens rea*.

c) John was possibly in a dazed condition when he made his late challenge on Kevin.

Issue: automatism, i.e. an external factor for some reason makes the defendant unable to control what he/she is doing. Lord Denning described it as something that is done by the muscles without any control of the mind, such as a spasm/relaxation, or an act done by a person who is not conscious of what he/she is doing, such as an act done while suffering from concussion.

John could be suffering from concussion due to the knock on the head he received, or his actions could have been done without any control of the mind. Therefore, his actions relate to automatism.

However, the defence is not available if the defendant's mind is still partially functioning (*Attorney General's Reference No 2*). The defendant must have total loss of control. Therefore, the defendant will need medical evidence to prove that his physical/mental state of mind at the time meant that he had no control over his actions and so was prevented from forming the *mens rea*. Therefore, John must provide evidence when using this defence. The courts must also consider insanity. If John can use the defence of automatism, this will mean he has no criminal liability for all of the non-fatal offences committed.

d) In his confused state, John thinks the referee is about to attack him and punches Gemma on the nose, causing it to bleed.

Issue: mistake as to self-defence. John believed he was about to be attacked. A defendant can use this defence if it appears that he honestly believed he was about to be attacked, and then used a degree of force that was reasonable in the context of what he perceived to be happening, as in *R* v *Williams*. The issue of what is reasonable force is left to the jury. So, if the jury believes that John honestly believed he was about to be attacked by Gemma, he could use the defence. Again, this will automatically result in a full acquittal.

This is a novel approach to answering the question, but one that allows the candidate to explore the major themes and issues. Such an approach may be beneficial to those who find it difficult to link the response to the question, or who need a systematic approach to formulate their responses. By identifying each element in turn, key issues can be discussed methodically. However, the response does not use this approach effectively and is disjointed.

The candidate would have benefited from a more detailed discussion of the non-fatal offences, explaining in more detail about the *actus reus* and *mens rea* elements with appropriate case law. The A-grade response, in comparison, focuses more on the explanation of critical elements and is stronger in terms of the AO2, due to the frequent application of the law to the scenario.

Question 7

Sean goes to his favourite corner store. In the shop he places some items of food in the wire shopping basket that is provided for shoppers. He also hides a small bottle of whisky in his coat pocket. He then removes the label from a high-priced CD that is in the charts, replaces it with the label from a specially reduced CD on the shelf below, and places the chart CD in the basket. He goes to the checkout and only pays for the items in the basket.

Outside the shop Sean sees a mountain bike that was there when he went in, and which he remembers seeing there at the same time the previous week. He rides home on it alongside a canal. On the way he notices a personal CD player on a table on board a canal longboat that is moored to the towpath. He climbs aboard and takes the CD player. He leaves the bike leaning against a fence at the end of his road and goes home.

Discuss Sean's criminal liability.

■ ■ ■

A-grade answer

This question involves issues of theft and burglary. These two offences are dealt with under the Theft Act 1968.

The offence of theft is dealt with under s.1(1). Theft is the dishonest appropriation of property belonging to another, with the intention to permanently deprive.

The first situation to look at is putting the whisky in his coat pocket. The whisky is clearly property satisfying s.4, as it is tangible property. Sean clearly satisfies s.3, appropriation, as he interferes with the rights of the owner by placing the bottle in his jacket. The whisky belongs to the supermarket, therefore satisfying s.5. Sean also had the intent to deprive and was dishonest according to *R v Ghosh*. This is therefore theft.

If we consider the CD, the key issue is that of appropriation. This is very similar to the case of *Morris*. In this case, the defendant had switched labels in a supermarket. He claimed he could not be guilty as he had not appropriated. He was convicted. This precedent will therefore apply and this defendant will be guilty of theft.

When Sean takes the bike this could amount to theft. The critical issues relate to his dishonesty and if the property is lost or abandoned.

Dishonesty is covered by s.2 of the Theft Act, which states that the defendant is not dishonest in certain situations. He may argue that under 2(1)(c) he is not dishonest. He may consider that the bike has been abandoned and that the owner cannot be found. In the case of *Small*, the defendant appropriated a car that he alleged had been abandoned. He claimed that the car had been in the same place for a week with the keys in the ignition. The Court of Appeal stated that there should be no conviction if the defendant honestly believed this. Applying this to Sean, he could argue that he had an honest belief that the owner could not be found, but this would be highly unlikely considering the differences between the situation in *Small* and the circumstances of Sean's offence.

Sean may also argue that he never intended to deprive the owner of the bike. This is covered by s.6. This section states that you intend to deprive permanently if you treat the property as your own and dispose of it regardless of the owner's rights. When he takes the bike and just leaves it, Sean is treating the property as his own. Therefore, he could not argue that he was not intending to deprive.

Sean then goes onto a canal boat and takes a CD player. This could be burglary. Section 9(1)(a) of the Theft Act 1968 states that a person will be guilty of burglary if he/she enters a building as a trespasser with the intention of committing an ulterior offence.

With regards entry, the case of *Ryan* states that entry does not have to be substantial or effective. Sean has clearly entered the houseboat. The houseboat will also need to be considered as a building. A building, according to case law and s.9(4), needs a degree of permanence or it can be an inhabited vessel. The canal boat would clearly be seen as a building.

When entering the building, Sean needs to be trespassing. Trespassing is a civil concept. In order to trespass, the defendant must enter the building intending to trespass or be reckless as to the trespass. Sean is obviously intending to trespass. He is entering a building that he has no permission to enter.

With regards to the *mens rea*, Sean needs to have the intent to commit an offence as specified in s.9 (2). With regards to this scenario, this will be theft. He notices the CD player before entering the boat and then climbs aboard and takes it. This will clearly satisfy the *mens rea* requirements of s.9(1)(a).

In conclusion, there is significant evidence that Sean can be convicted of theft and burglary.

🖉 This response has a methodical structure. The candidate discusses the key issues in the question in turn — taking the whisky, switching the labels, taking the bike and taking the CD player from the canal boat. This is a good approach as it allows a discussion in manageable chunks and means that the candidate does not miss anything out.

The candidate uses the facts of the scenario to highlight and strengthen the discussion. He/she also uses a good blend of statute and case law to support and add depth to the AO1, and only highlights and adds detail to those areas critical to the question. This is important in problem questions due to the range of issues involved. Although there are certain cases missing, e.g. *Hinks*, the breadth of issues and the range of discussion clearly show wide-ranging knowledge.

■ ■ ■

C-grade answer

This case involved theft. Theft is introduced in s.1(1) of the Theft Act 1968. It creates the offence of theft. It states that a person is guilty of theft if he/she dishonestly appropriates property belonging to another with the intention of permanently depriving the other of it. Theft is triable either way. The maximum punishment that can be imposed, where a defendant has been convicted of theft following trial on indictment, was reduced from 10 years by the Criminal Justice Act 1991.

Section 3 states that any assumption of the rights of the owner amounts to an appropriation and this includes, where he has come by the property without stealing it, any later assumptions of a right to it by keeping it as an owner. The definition given in *Gomez* is very wide and the Court of Appeal tried to modify the scope in the cases of *Gallasso* and *Mazo*. The House of Lords confirmed the breadth of appropriations in the case of *R* v *Hinks*. In *Hinks*, the victim was a 53-year-old man of limited intelligence who had been left money by his father. The defendant had befriended the man and was alleged by the prosecution to have encouraged him to withdraw £60,000 from his building society account and deposit it into her own. The defendant was guilty. The House of Lords held that a valid gift could be an appropriation, i.e. keeping, dealing and expectation for bona fide purchasers.

Appropriation is done by Sean when he hides a small bottle of whisky in his coat pocket. However, when Sean appropriates, he may not have the state of mind needed for theft. This can cause, and has caused, the courts problems — when he interferes with the rights of the owner he will not have the *mens rea* for theft. There is a legal principle stating that the *actus reus* and the *mens rea* must coincide. It is important to consider if an appropriation is an immediate act or whether it continues over time. The court decided in *Atakpu and Abrahams* that appropriation is a continuing act. Therefore, Sean will not be able to argue that his *actus reus* and *mens rea* do not match.

Sean will satisfy the other *actus reus* elements. The whisky is clearly property under the definition given in s.4, and under s.5 it belongs to the supermarket that owns it. For the *mens rea* aspect of theft, Sean will have to be dishonest and also intend to permanently deprive the shop of the whisky.

The 1968 Act only provides guidance on what is not dishonesty. Section 2(1) illustrates three situations that are not deemed dishonest, i.e. if someone appropriates property in the belief that he/she has, in law, the right to deprive the other of it, he/she is not dishonest. These three situations are not applicable to Sean.

For example, in the case of *Powell* v *McRae*, the defendant was a turnstile operator at Wembley Stadium who dishonestly accepted £2 from a member of the public. He admitted the person, even though he was fully aware that entrance was by ticket only. He was convicted of the £2 theft.

The courts will have to apply the Ghosh test on dishonesty. This will consider whether the ordinary, reasonable person would consider Sean dishonest, and then consider if Sean himself would have realised his own dishonesty.

These principles on theft, if applied to the bike and the CD, will also make Sean guilty of the theft offence.

Boarding the canal boat without permission can be seen as burglary. Section 9 involves entering a building without permission with the intention of committing a number of offences. The relevant offence in this scenario is theft, as Sean has taken a CD player. The key issue is whether the boat can be classed as a building. Vessels that are inhabited are considered to be buildings, e.g. a caravan.

Entry is discussed in the cases of *Collins*, *Brown* and *Ryan*. The test of entry has changed significantly in these cases. Originally, entry needed to be substantial and effective, but the lead case of *Ryan* means that entry need not fulfil these criteria.

The issue of trespass is discussed in *Collins*. According to this case, the defendant is a trespasser if he/she intends to trespass or is reckless about the trespass.

To conclude, Sean is guilty of theft and burglary.

The candidate has covered all the key elements. The response uses the Theft Act sections to support its arguments, although more detail should have been included, for example on the intention to permanently deprive. While some cases are mentioned, the overall use of case law could be improved. Some cases used are not made relevant to the question, e.g. the description of *Powell* v *McRae*.

Problem-style questions require an application of the law, and this varies throughout the response. The discussion on dishonesty is of a good standard, but the discussion of the bike and the CD has no depth. Candidates must remember that AO2 is worth 20 marks and cannot be neglected.

Section C

Question 8

Archie is owed £50 by Brett. Archie sees Brett in the street and threatens to beat Brett up unless he pays the £50 then and there. Brett does give Archie the money. Archie walks on and sees an old lady, Charlotte, carrying a handbag. Archie tries to snatch the bag by grabbing the handle. Charlotte tries to keep hold of the bag. The bag falls to the ground and Archie runs off.

Evaluate the accuracy of each of the four statements A, B, C and D individually, as they apply to the facts in the above scenario.

Statement A: Archie is not liable for theft because Brett gave him the £50.
Statement B: Archie is not liable for robbery when Brett gives him the £50.
Statement C: Archie is not liable for the theft of Charlotte's handbag.
Statement D: Archie is guilty of robbery when he snatches Charlotte's handbag.

A-grade answer

Statement A

The statement is not true because an appropriation can take place even where there is consent by the owner. In any case any consent here is invalid because it is only gained under threat. Even though Archie may have an honest belief that he is owed the money he cannot get it back in this way.

Statement B

Robbery is theft with force or the threat of force used before or at the time of the theft in order to steal. Archie has used the threat of force to make Brett hand over the £50. Even though Brett has given Archie the money this does not mean Archie is innocent, and even though Archie may genuinely feel that he is owed the money it is still robbery and the statement is inaccurate.

Statement C

The statement is inaccurate. Archie can be convicted of theft. This is because any assumption of the rights of an owner can amount to appropriation. So when Archie grabs the handle of the bag this is enough for theft and it does not matter that the bag falls to the floor and Archie runs away.

Statement D

Again, robbery is theft where the defendant before or at the time of the theft uses force or the threat of force in order to steal. Decided case law has established that force being applied to property is sufficient for robbery. On this basis Archie has appropriated the bag and has used force to do it.

> 🖉 This is an excellent answer. The candidate has identified the key elements in relation to each statement and has reasoned accurately for a high Level 5 mark.

C-grade answer

Statement A
Archie is owed £50 by Brett and is given £50 by Brett. Although Archie did threaten Brett with violence, if he genuinely believed that he is owed the money and honestly believes he can get the money in this way he is not guilty as in a decided case. Archie is not liable for theft because he is given the money by Brett and therefore it is not dishonest. He may be guilty of robbery, however.

Statement B
Archie used the threat of force when he took the money back that he is owed by Brett. Therefore it looks as though this is a burglary. However, if Archie genuinely believed that he is entitled to obtain the money in this way he is not guilty of robbery. This comes from a similar case.

Statement C
Archie is guilty of theft when he grabs Charlotte's handbag. He has completed the dishonest appropriation of property belonging to another person with an intention to permanently deprive. When the handbag fell to the floor the appropriation was complete, although Archie is more likely to be charged with the more serious crime of robbery. Therefore the statement is not accurate.

Statement D
Archie did use force when he attempted to appropriate the handbag. Under *Clouden*, snatching the handbag can be classed as force. Although Archie dropped the handbag and ran away without it, the appropriation was complete the moment the handbag hit the floor.

The answers are mixed here: some reasonable and one good but one weak. The candidate has made a basic point with some reasoning for A but is off the point somewhat. For B the candidate has mistakenly referred to burglary rather than robbery in the first instance but has reasoned correctly on the use of force and has some good reasoning also on Archie's intention. For C the candidate possibly only needed to identify that any assumption of the rights of an owner is an appropriation to move into Level 5. Otherwise it was a good answer. Finally for D the candidate only needed to develop the reasoning more to gain a higher mark. Overall, though, an adequate answer.